From Geography
to Affinity

From Geography to Affinity

How Congregations Can Learn from One Another

Lyle E. Schaller

Abingdon Press

Nashville

FROM GEOGRAPHY TO AFFINITY
HOW CONGREGATIONS CAN LEARN FROM ONE ANOTHER

Library of Congress Cataloging-in-Publication Data

Schaller, Lyle E.
  From geography to affinity : how congregations can learn from one another / Lyle E. Schaller.
      p.   cm.
  ISBN 0-687-02266-5 (pbk. : alk. paper)
  1. Church work. 2. Christian sects. I. Title.

  BV652.S2925 2003
  280'.4'0973—dc21

                                                                      2003004501

03 04 05 06 07 08 09 10 11 12—10 9 8 7 6 5 4 3 2 1

MANUFACTURED IN THE UNITED STATES OF AMERICA

To
Virgil Bjork
Don LaSuer
Elvin Miller
Ray Sells

CONTENTS

INTRODUCTION

What is the future of those predominantly white mainline Protestant denominations in America?[1] One set of forecasts sees a continued numerical decline and a diminishing proportion of that growing number of Protestant churchgoers affiliated with these mainline denominations.

A significant number of these pessimists point to the shrinking numbers as a symptom, rather than as a source of despair. They contend the number-one reason for their pessimism is the denominational agenda. They fondly recall when their denominational agenda and the ordering of priorities was organized around a single unifying theme. This is how we will work together to fulfill the Great Commission. They defend their current pessimism by contending that in recent years the agenda of their denomination has been organized around either (a) presenting a report and recommendation that is guaranteed to polarize the constituency and/or (b) housekeeping concerns such as a better pension system for pastors or restructuring the denomination or ecumenism or a proposed merger with another denomination or appeals for more money or funding institutions founded decades earlier.

A far more optimistic scenario is projected by those, including this observer, who are convinced the best years for these mainline Protestant denominations may be in the twenty-first century.

What are the central differences between these two sets of expectations? The pessimists doubt that the policymakers will make the changes required to reach, attract, serve, nurture, assimilate, challenge, and persuade the generations of Americans born after 1960 of the validity and relevance of the gospel of Jesus Christ. The pessimists are convinced these aging mainline Protestant denominations are driven by tradition and a dream of recreating yesteryear. The pessimists are convinced the new religious movements in the United States will replace these old mainline Protestant denominations.

Those of us who are more optimistic about the future are convinced God raises up the leaders needed at every stage of the history of the Christian church. We are heartened by that small, but growing group of leaders who are not simply open to new ideas, but more important, are creating new ways to reach new generations and recent immigrants with the good news of Jesus Christ. We are encouraged by the surveys that indicate the increase in worship attendance by white Protestants in America has matched and perhaps exceeded the rate of population growth in the United States since 1950. We are thrilled with what appears to be an unprecedented number of teenagers on a serious personal religious pilgrimage. We are impressed by the vitality of contemporary Christian ministries on college and university campuses. We are especially encouraged by that huge number of churchgoers who describe how their life has been transformed by the challenge to be engaged in doing ministry, to do what they knew they could never do. A big source of our optimism is based on that growing number of American Protestant congregations that have moved beyond "taking care of and serving our constituents" to focusing on the transformation of lives through meaningful and memorable experiences. We also are greatly encouraged by that new generation of parish pastors and paid program staff members born after about 1952 who are transforming the nature of the parish ministry.

In summary, the pessimists appear to be convinced change is unlikely and perpetuating past organizational structures, policies, and practices inevitably will produce continued numerical decline.

Most of the optimists agree that rejecting change does lead to institutional obsolescence, but we are encouraged by that growing number of policymakers in the mainline denominations who already are initiating the changes required to create a new tomorrow. The most highly visible examples are the pastors, program staff, and volunteer leaders in that growing number of very large mainline Protestant congregations that have doubled or tripled or quadrupled their worship attendance since 1990.

Most of them are comfortable with the products of twentieth century technological advances such as cheap and universally available electricity, radio, the privately owned motor vehicle, air-conditioning, motion pictures, color slides, television, commercial air travel, thermostats, public address systems, recorded music, copy machines, computers, cordless microphones, coffeemakers, e-mail, color printers, Web sites, LCD projectors, and the broadband.

A smaller, and younger, but growing number are adjusting to the fact that projected visual images and music are replacing the spoken word and the printed word as primary channels of human communication. (Touch continues to be number one, however.)

The optimists also are encouraged that the demand for high quality and relevant preaching and teaching probably is at an all-time high.

A Third Perspective

A third perspective insists the crucial distinction is not between the pessimists and the optimists. This perspective declares the most important line of demarcation is between those committed to perpetuating old institutions, old systems, and the old ways of "how to do church" and those creative and entrepreneurial individuals who prefer to focus on giving birth to the new.

Efforts to perpetuate the old naturally tend to generate pessimism, frustration, and despair. By contrast, efforts to create the new tend to be based on an optimistic view of the future. These efforts also tend to be driven by passion and to generate excitement. Failures do occur, but they are soon overshadowed by the excitement created when others exceed the original expectations.

This perspective is articulated by the scores of parish pastors and the thousands of deeply committed lay volunteers who have walked away from the frustrations evoked by efforts to perpetuate or reform the old. They have volunteered to go out and help give birth to the new, often in new nondenominational missions.

At this point the reader may interrupt and ask, "If that is true, why write a book on renewing the old? Why not write a book on inventing the new?"

Why This Book?

Those are two relevant questions and they deserve a response. First, dozens of excellent books already have been written about inventing the new.[2] Second, at least a few million of us have such a deep loyalty to our own religious tradition that we cannot abandon it for greener pastures. Since they were married in 1970 the husband has held sixteen jobs in twelve states. He was fired from fourteen of the sixteen. He may be a failure in that competitive labor market, but he has been a faithful and loving husband, a kind and responsible parent, and a thoughtful son-in-law. Why doesn't his wife abandon him? Because she loves him!

Third, most of us believe our denomination is filled with a huge quantity of assets. That long list includes devout and hardworking pastors, dedicated lay volunteers, faithful members, responsible denominational staff, money, real estate, and hundreds or thousands of vital congregations. Good stewardship prohibits abandoning those assets.

Each one of the seven largest of what often are lumped together as "the old mainline Protestant denominations in

America" is larger in members and worshipers than 90 percent of all organized religious bodies in the United States that have a national headquarters. Each one represents a huge quantity of accumulated resources.

Fourth, and most influential, the Christian faith is a religion that generates hope among the believers.[3] If the only real problem is a dysfunctional system, why not redesign the system? One answer is that it is far easier to create the new than to renew the old. A better answer, however, is with God all things are possible.

A fifth reason to write this book is to advocate a relatively easy approach to planned change initiated from within an organization. One way to proclaim the gospel of Jesus Christ in contemporary America is for a team of three-to-seven deeply devoted Christians to design and plant a new nondenominational church. They are free of institutional traditions, precedents, rules, laws, and policies. They are free to mobilize the resources required to implement a vision of a new tomorrow rather than to attempt to replicate the old.

A different approach selects and builds on relevant traditions and precedents. This approach affirms the best of those traditions and precedents, restates them to fit the contemporary environment, and builds on them. The strategy suggested in this book is based on three paradigm shifts, but each is really a restatement of the old.

The central theme calls for congregations to be free to choose their affiliation with a midlevel judicatory on the basis of affinity, not geography. This parallels the criteria millions of church shoppers use as they choose a new church home. Instead of organizing on the basis of the geographical location of the meeting place, they join with others who share a major point of commonality. That is an old American concept. That is a central organizing principle in every one of the mainline Protestant denominations in America. Synods, dioceses, conferences, districts, presbyteries, and regions are not designed to bring together all of the Christians, or even all the Christian congregations in that community. They are organized around a point of commonality called a denominational heritage. Geographical proximity is only the second of these organizing principles in defining the membership of a regional judicatory.

In recent years thousands of mainline American Protestant congregations have minimized those two central organizing principles by joining a nongeographical and nondenominational affinity network where the congregational leaders see they have much in common with other churches in that network. The Leadership Network, the Willow Creek Association, and Churches United in Global Mission are only three of those non-geographical and nondenominational networks.

This book recommends giving congregations the option of affiliating with intradenominational and nongeographical judicatories. That represents a more conservative paradigm shift than abandoning the denominational tie completely. Thousands of new churches have chosen the more radical shift of relating only to a nongeographical and nondenominational affinity network. Which of these alternative scenarios will strengthen your denomination?

A second, and more modest paradigm shift is discussed in chapter 5. This is relatively new in the church, but old in the rest of the economy. How do people learn? Do they learn best in a superior-subordinate design such as boss-employee or teacher-student or leader-follower relationship? Or is peer learning more effective? The large American law firms, teenagers, teaching hospitals, golfers, amateur gardeners, new neighbors, women recovering from a painful divorce, graduate schools, and new mothers are examples of that growing affirmation of the power of peer learning.

Where can congregational leaders go to learn how to do church effectively in twenty-first century America? To theological seminaries? To denominationally sponsored workshops? To continuing education events led by experts? This paradigm shift suggests the most productive are peer-learning experiences with the paid and volunteer staff of teaching churches. These also can be designed to reinforce intradenominational cohesion and loyalty as secondary objectives.

The third paradigm shift (chapter 11) is offered as a response to the erosion of institutional loyalties, the replacement of neighborhood institutions by larger regional institutions, and the hazards that go with building the public image of any organization around the personality and gifts of a particular individual. Leaders come and go.

Therefore instead of building the public image of a congregation around the real estate or denominational label or the social class of the members or the pastor, this book recommends building that community image around that congregation's distinctive role in ministry. That also is not a new idea, but it is widely ignored.

In other words, one reason for writing this book is to suggest that the renewal of a denominational system not only is possible, it can be accomplished by building on what in fact are old patterns. This is NOT based on new and untested theories of how the world should be.

One of the most influential reasons for writing this book is the conviction that denominations are legitimate orders of God's creation. Many will disagree with that statement. My conviction is based on the writings of Paul who repeatedly affirms the concept of the interdependence of Christian congregations. Denominations can provide a healthy and challenging structure for expressing that interdependence. The details of that organizational structure must be customized to fit the time and the place. The big risk, of course, is for that institution to see itself as the end in itself, rather than as a means-to-an-end. This risk is enhanced by the temptation of the leaders in any institution to identify themselves as the essence of that institution rather than as servants of the constituents. Political scientists have identified that as a common pattern among dictatorships. Napoleon in France, Hitler in Germany, and Castro in Cuba are examples. Any effort to reform the institution is perceived as an attack on the person in charge.

On the ecclesiastical scene one of the most memorable signs in front of a church building reads, "Independent Presbyterian

Church." That is an oxymoron! By definition a Presbyterian congregation should affirm the interdependence of the churches.

One option in contemporary American Protestantism is for an independent Christian congregation to ignore all other churches and unilaterally design and implement its own ministry without any relationship with or accountability to other churches. A second is to affiliate with a nondenominational affinity network in order to learn from one another and/or to cooperate with others in that network to design and carry out a few specialized ministries. This is clearly the growing pattern in American Christianity today.

A third alternative, which this book recommends, is to undergird and strengthen the role of denominations by enabling congregations to create and affiliate with intradenominational and nongeographical affinity judicatories. Instead of abandoning denominational systems, redesign and strengthen them.

Finally, why write it now? The ideal time to replace that old battery in your car is not on a cold Sunday morning in January as the car fails to start when you turn the key in the switch. The best time was the previous August. The best time to reinvent your denominational system may have been in 1973, but at that time no one believed it was necessary. People tend to be more receptive to change when there is a widely shared perception, "We are facing a crisis." Today denial has been replaced in most denominational circles by a reluctant admission, "Our old system isn't working as effectively as it did two or three decades ago." While it may not be the ideal lifestyle, millions of people postpone a trip to the dentist until they have a toothache. A lot of denominational teeth are hurting today.

Those are seven reasons to explain the decision to write this book. Should you read this book? That is a relevant question and the first chapter offers a dozen reasons why you might decide that would be a waste of your time. That chapter concludes with a brief summary of a dozen assumptions on which this book is based. (A few of my old friends will be delighted to discover that I have agreed twelve is a better number than forty-four.)

The second chapter is based on the conviction that the road to planned change initiated from within an organization often begins with the need for people to talk with one another about contemporary reality. One theme for those early discussions calls for reaching agreement on what we believe (chapter 3) and on the consequences of affluence replacing scarcity in the American economy (chapter 4).

The fifth chapter describes the emergence of the self-identified teaching church—that second paradigm shift to peer learning.

The sixth chapter is an attempt to shift the focus in planning from precedents and input, such as budgets and personnel, to identifying the desired outcomes. If your denominational system is not producing the desired outcomes, what changes are needed in your system? Could one of these be in the polity? (See chapter 7.) Or could it be the frame of reference used to define the system? (See chapter 8.)

The ninth chapter finally gets to the heart of the issue and describes a variety of actual and potential affinity judicatories.

The tenth chapter is intended for those readers who reject the idea of offering congregations a choice between affiliation either with the traditional geographically defined regional judicatory or with a nongeographical affinity judicatory and demand, "What are the other options for fulfilling the Great Commission?" Twelve alternatives are described.

As mentioned earlier, a third paradigm shift is described in a brief eleventh chapter.

The twelfth chapter is offered for those thoughtful people who recognize every action produces consequences. Systems do produce the outcomes they are designed to produce. Those outcomes include both desired and unanticipated consequences. Several of these are discussed in the last chapter.

The most interesting of these, which because of this writer's ignorance is not included, can be summarized in a question. What will the policymakers of 2035 agree will be the best way to organize their denomination for the middle third of the twenty-first century? Affinity judicatories could turn out to be simply a bridge between the old and the really new.

Finally, brief appendixes summarize seven sets of statistical data that are designed to help the readers define contemporary reality and to identify a few of the differences among various religious traditions in America.

Scores of dedicated Christians who have shared their concerns, hopes, and dreams for their denomination are responsible for many of the insights, questions, and thoughts in this book, but they are too numerous to be identified individually. I am grateful for their ideas, but any blame for errors of fact or interpretation rests solely on this observer.

CHAPTER ONE

SHOULD YOU READ THIS BOOK?

Your time is valuable! Should you spend a couple of hours of that scarce and irreplaceable resource reading this book? The best answer to this question can be found by reflecting on a dozen diagnostic statements about today and tomorrow. If you agree with at least nine or ten, and the first four in particular, it probably would be a waste of your time to read this book.

1. You are convinced the institutional and spiritual health of your denominational tradition is excellent. Your congregations are vital, healthy, and effective in reaching new generations of American-born residents as well as recent immigrants to America. Your denominational systems are producing the outcomes you desire and should not be changed.

2. Every congregation in American Protestantism should

define itself as a geographical parish committed to reaching and serving the residents who live within a mile or two (or perhaps seven miles in rural areas with a low population density) of their meeting place. We also believe that instead of encouraging congregations to focus on a relatively homogeneous segment of the population, every worshiping community should consist of a representative cross section of the people living within that congregation's service area. One component of a larger strategy to achieve those two goals is a geographical definition of the churches to be served by our midlevel regional judicatories.

3. We believe a primary responsibility of congregations is to resource denominational systems by sending money and volunteer leadership. By contrast, this book suggests the primary role of the midlevel judicatories is to enhance the capability of congregations to fulfill the Great Commission. We disagree! Our congregations now enjoy an unprecedented array of vendors who are both competent and eager to provide customized resourcing on every concern from teaching materials to counsel on capital-funds campaigns to community outreach ministries to the design of worship experiences to music. That frees our denominational system to concentrate on other issues, and we find the geographically defined regional judicatory a useful and inclusive structure for fulfilling that role.

4. You are convinced that the mainline American Protestant denominations of the last half of the twentieth century are terminally ill. Proposals that suggest the future will bring the best of times for these denominations are naively optimistic. They belong in the same category as efforts to recreate the family farm of 1947 or the five-and-ten-cent variety store on Main Street of 1950 or the small public high school of 1955 or the four-bedroom single-family house with a one-car garage constructed in 1958.

The schisms that created the Presbyterian Church in America in 1973 and the Evangelical Presbyterian Church in 1981, plus the more recent withdrawals of congregations from the Evangelical Lutheran Church in America, the Southern Baptist Convention, the United Church of Christ, the Episcopal Church, and other denominations demonstrate it is too late to design a wider and more inclusive tent. Culture is more powerful than denominational loyalties, and culture in American religion has become a highly divisive force. In other words, you are convinced it is too late for the renewal of old denominational systems.

5. Affirming the creation and operation of affinity judicatories requires granting lay leadership in general and local leadership in particular for greater authority and responsibility than our clergy-dominated system would ever approve. Furthermore, you are convinced that denominational systems should and do carry the primary responsibility for fulfilling the Great Commission. Congregations have a secondary role in fulfilling the Great Commission. Therefore why waste time studying a design that will be politically unacceptable in our religious tradition?

6. While you are experiencing a few problems as a result of the erosion of denominational loyalty by the generations born between 1940–80, you are confident the pendulum is about to swing. You are confident the generations born after 1980 will display the same high level of institutional loyalty as those born in the first third of the twentieth century.

7. This book missed the boat! The top agenda item for the mainline Protestant denominations during the next quarter century will be how to produce reasonably friendly schisms and minimize litigation. We all know the best way to predict tomorrow for the Lutherans, Methodists, and others is to look at what the Presbyterians began to do twenty years ago. The issue is how to respond to schismatic forces, and this book does not deal with that, so why waste time reading it? (That is NOT an accurate statement! One theme of this book is how to avoid the pressures for schism.)

8. You are convinced that within a few years the United States government and most states will replace the income tax with a tax on carbon emissions. One consequence will be a huge increase in the cost of gasoline that will restore the viability of neighborhood institutions and geographically defined denominational structures.

9. The distrust of institutions is increasing. The big contemporary example is the crisis in the Roman Catholic Church in America. One consequence is distrust of long-tenured leadership. The adoption of the Twenty-second Amendment to the United States Constitution in 1951, that limited the tenure of the president of the United States to two full terms, is one example. You believe the best antidote to distrust is short tenure. This book encourages long-term relationships and long tenure for pastors and denominational leaders, so why read it?

10. Your experience is that congregations subsidized by the dead (endowment funds) and/or by the denomination usually are more vital and more effective in fulfilling the Great Commission than are those churches that are fully self-financing.

11. You are convinced the policy-formulation and decision-making processes of your denomination should be driven by (a) precedents, (b) inputs such as budgets, (c) providing jobs for adults, and (d) ideology, not as this book recommends, by desired outcomes.

12. The ecumenical movement has been winning increasing support among the mainline Protestant denominations for more than forty years. If the recommendations in this book are implemented, one consequence will be a strengthening of denominational systems and an enhancement of the loyalty congregations feel toward their denomination. That is incompatible with encouraging greater interdenominational cooperation. Given a choice, you prefer to promote Christian unity rather than strengthen denominational systems. (Note: Some readers will disagree with this either-or view. They believe that ecumenism flourishes among large, strong, numerically growing, healthy, and vital congregations and denominations.)

If most of these twelve statements represent your view of the future of the mainline Protestant denominations in America, you already have wasted too much of your valuable time.

A Dozen Assumptions

On the other hand, if you disagree with most or all of those twelve statements, you may want to explore the basic assumptions on which this book rests.

1. God has not written off the future of denominational systems in America. The best years may be in the future. God has given us the freedom to make that decision. That God-given freedom to individuals has been enlarged by changes in the American economy, the political system, and the culture since 1776.[1]

2. The competition among the Christian churches in the United States to reach, invite, attract, serve, challenge, assimilate, and nurture younger generations is far greater than ever before. In other words, the call to the churches in the twenty-first century is not only to be faithful and obedient, but also to be relevant and competitive. The family-owned and operated general store in the village of 200 residents in 1935 was a friendly environment that offered a high level of customer service, but it cannot compete with today's 200,000-square-foot superstore on a twenty-acre site.

3. Systems produce the outcomes they are designed to produce. One widely shared worldview is, "Things just happen." This book is based on the conviction that W. Edwards Deming was right. Slogans, quotas, shame, guilt, high-powered rhetoric, and fear no longer are effective in improving the performance of an organization.[2]

When old systems become counterproductive or fail to produce the desired outcomes, they should be replaced! That is the big challenge before American leaders in the Roman Catholic Church.

4. A new system for these mainline Protestant denominations should place a high priority on (a) resourcing congregations, (b) giving birth to the new, (c) facilitating the transformation of believers into devoted disciples of Jesus Christ,

and (d) encouraging the emergence of more very large congregations that are able to mobilize the resources required to provide the quality, relevance, and choices sought by younger generations.[3] A much lower priority should be placed on (a) perpetuating old institutions, (b) regulating congregational life, and (c) taking care of the clergy. One of the most difficult assignments is to renew an old and obsolete institution. It is much easier and more rewarding to create the new. The creation of tax-funded charter schools is one example of that guideline.

5. More people than ever before in world history believe they have the right to determine their future and to choose from among a variety of attractive alternatives in designing their own future. "For the first time—and I mean that literally—substantial and rapidly growing numbers of people have choices. For the first time, people have had to *manage themselves*. And we are totally unprepared for it." [See "Foreword" by Peter Drucker in Bob Buford, *Stuck In Halftime* (Grand Rapids, Mich., 2001), p. 9. Drucker describes this as the most important event on this planet in our time.]

6. There is still time to transform the culture and the institutional systems of these denominations, but it will not be easy!

One reason is most of the people in these mainline Protestant denominations do not feel a sense of crisis. Most are convinced, "My denomination will be here long after I'm dead, so why worry? Why push for change?" They are right. Denial is more comfortable than change.

While there is widespread agreement that the recent and current outcomes have had a minimal overlap with the desired outcomes, nothing resembling a consensus exists in regard to a renewal strategy. That road to renewal is filled with many barriers.

The highest barrier may be denial. There is nothing wrong with the system. All that is required is either (a) a bigger hammer or (b) better people to run the system.

Second, in several mainline Protestant denominations there is an absence of agreement on the primary role of the denomination and on the top two or three priorities in the allocation of resources.

A third big barrier is legal. The present systems were designed to make it exceptionally difficult for those who want to amend, revise, renew, or scrap the old system. Those dead white males of the eighteenth, nineteenth, and early twentieth centuries realized the churchgoers of the twenty-first century could not be trusted! They designed several high legal barriers to change.

Fourth, a lot of highly influential denominational leaders have committed their futures to perpetuating the present system. Replacing the present obsolete and dysfunctional systems would place hundreds of jobs in jeopardy.

Fifth, the decision-making systems in these denominations have been designed to make it easy to reject proposals for change and tempting to look for compromises that can win broad-based support.

Sixth, and perhaps the most widely neglected factor is most denominational systems do not include a system of accountability based on an annual audit of performance as measured by actual outcomes.

7. We know what to do and how to do it. It is not necessary to begin with a blank sheet of paper and dream up new systems. The ecclesiastical landscape in America is covered with (a) hundreds of congregations that are modeling how to do ministry in the twenty-first century with new generations of younger American-born residents on a self-identified religious pilgrimage and (b) several denominational systems that are modeling the concept of affinity midlevel judicatories. The call is not to invent a new wheel. The call is to replace that worn-out or broken wheel with a better wheel that already has been invented and is in use.

8. The arrival of the age of affluence in the post–World War II era has transformed the context for ministry. (See chapter 4.)

9. The three paradigm shifts suggested in this book are really conservative. One is to replace an input-driven planning model that focuses on money, personnel, schedules, regulation, traditions, governance, and real estate with a process that emphasizes desired outcomes. Another is to at least offer congregations the opportunity to be members of learning-driven affinity networks and judicatories. The third is to recognize that role and ministry are more

significant components of a congregation's community identity than denominational affiliation. (See chapters 5, 7, and 11.)

10. The issue is not a choice between change and perpetuating the past! One of the questions at the heart of this issue is whether congregations should be encouraged to look to intradenominational affinity judicatories for resourcing or to continue to turn to "outside" parachurch organizations, teaching churches, and a score of other sources for help.

11. It also should be emphasized a switch to affinity judicatories is not the only possible course of action. That is the easiest and most promising. A dozen more difficult strategies are identified in chapter 10.

12. Finally, the two key assumptions in this book are (a) in a world of increasing complexity and greater competition, congregations need customized ministry plans and (b) the most effective way to create a customized ministry plan is for congregational leaders to go and learn from churches that currently are implementing a strategy that could be adapted to fit their church. Those are two of the key components of a strategy to fulfill the Great Commission.

If you agree most of those assumptions are consistent with contemporary reality, the next step may be to encourage the policymakers in your denomination to talk about what your system is producing and to compare actual outcomes with the desired outcomes.

CHAPTER TWO

WHY TALK ABOUT IT?

For several generations Protestants in America have been comfortable talking about the Roman Catholic Church in the United States. This has become a widespread practice since January 2002 when the press began to provide Americans with details about a crisis in the Roman Catholic Church. The crisis provides leaders in the mainline American Protestant church with a useful case study. It is now clear that the system for producing priests for the Roman Catholic Church in America was designed to produce a variety of outcomes. That list of outcomes includes (1) only unmarried males will be ordained, (2) only rarely will ordained ministers from Protestant denominations be ordained to the Catholic priesthood, (3) nearly all the adult role models in that educational process will be never-married males, (4) the number of priests ordained each year will be fewer than the number of replacements required for that year, (5) a disproportionately large number of men will be ordained who are not sexually mature or who are sexually maladjusted,

(6) a disproportionately large number of allegations will be made of incidents of the sexual abuse of children and youth by priests, (7) substantial financial payments will be made to victims of this abuse by dozens of dioceses while other victims will receive no financial compensation, (8) a disproportionately large number of Catholic priests in America will be gay men, (9) the nature of that hierarchical organizational structure will tempt persons in positions of authority to deny or cover up or conceal the problem, including their own conduct, (10) eventually the combination of investigative reporting, which became popular in America in the 1960s, plus the financial rewards for tort lawyers, will produce a major public scandal when the historical record is uncovered, (11) the level of trust of the constituents in the institutional expression of their religion will be severely eroded, and (12) millions of lifelong American Catholics will leave the Roman Catholic Church.

One defensive explanation was, "No one planned for this to happen. These were not the outcomes the leaders of the church desired. These outcomes just happened." That represents a harsh indictment of the leaders who designed and operated that system. It suggests they were incompetent or naive or stupid or guilty of malpractice. That defense suggests the leaders who designed and operated the system were concerned only with inputs and did not consider a full range of probable outcomes.

The Law of Unintended Consequences

A better defense is based on the law of unintended consequences. This ancient bit of wisdom recognizes that every system, no matter how carefully designed, will produce unanticipated and often undesired outcomes. This law guides the decision-making processes in the practice of medicine, in farming, in transportation, in church planning, in education, and in raising governmental revenues through taxation.

Three common examples can be seen in the application of this law in the churches. One is the desired outcomes that accompany long pastorates often produce difficulties for the successor when that long-tenured minister disappears from the scene after a twenty-to-forty year pastorate. A second is rapid numerical growth in a congregation often is accompanied by an increase in the level of anonymity and the degree of complexity. A third is hiring staff from among the members usually produces many desired outcomes, but it may produce difficulties if the day comes when that staff person is unwillingly dismissed.

The standard response to the law of unintended consequences includes (1) raising the level of competence for internal self-criticism and (2) installing a continuing internal system of monitoring all inputs with special sensitivity to early identification of unanticipated outcomes. This is relatively easy to do in an institution with a relatively flat organizational structure. It is much more difficult to install and activate in a highly centralized and hierarchical multilayer organizational structure designed to reward obedience and loyalty to those in high positions in that hierarchy. This explains why a longtime friend congratulated a newly elected Protestant bishop and added, "And this means you never again will hear the truth about your preaching."

One of the many barriers to reform in the Roman Catholic Church in America was the provision in the canon law that declared a priest could not be laicized without approval from the Vatican. A second was that in many states the law did not require the authorities in any religious organization to report allegations of the sexual abuse of children to public law enforcement agencies. American public policy made it easier to carry out the cover-up.

The big barrier to reform in the Roman Catholic Church in America, however, was that standard response to the law of unintended consequences failed. The capability for internal and constructive self-criticism was inadequate. Monitoring systems existed and they did raise red flags. These included reports in 1985 and 1992–93 received by all American bishops. The second warned of the coming of the biggest crisis for the Roman Catholic Church since the Protestant Reformation.

The warnings were largely ignored. The law of unintended consequences prevailed. For months American newspapers, television stations, religious journals, and news magazines have described in great detail the unintended consequences of a system that produced both desired and undesirable consequences.

What Is the First Lesson?

The mainline Protestant denominations in America are not exempt from the law of unintended consequences. One example is the system that calls for one minister to serve concurrently as the pastor of two or three small congregations has turned out to be an effective means for closing or merging small congregations. In these mergers five plus three usually ends up equaling somewhere between three and six, not eight.

Denominational mergers often are advocated as part of a larger goal under the umbrella of Christian unity. Unintended consequences usually include (1) a decrease in the number of congregations, (2) a cutback in new church development, (3) a decrease in membership, (4) an increase in the median age of the constituency, and (5) a decrease in "market share" or proportion of the American population affiliated with that successor denomination.

The key lesson to be gleaned from the recent experiences of the Roman Catholic Church in America, however, is not to dwell on the law of unintended consequences. The key lesson is the value of (1) an institutional capability for internal self-criticism, (2) a sophisticated system for monitoring the actual outcomes from that specific religious organizational system, and (3) the capability and willingness of the official leadership to receive and use the warnings supplied by that monitoring system on revising and improving the operation of that system.

That does not happen automatically!

The Presbyterian Church (U.S.A.), for example, enjoys the benefits of a superb research agency in its national headquarters in Louisville. It would be a gross exaggeration, however, to suggest that monitoring process has transformed the operational systems of the General Assembly, the synods, or the presbyteries.

The last three decades of the twentieth century brought the publication of literally hundreds of reports, books, studies, and essays by task forces, scholars, denominational staff members, committees, commissions, pastors, lay groups, and others warning that the current operational systems of the mainline denominations were producing undesired outcomes. An excellent summary of much of this research was published in 1996. Three of the many significant conclusions in this report were presented in single sentences. "Congregations, rather than denominations, have become the primary mission organizations of American mainstream Protestantism."[1] "We mainstream Protestants cannot control or determine the moral values of this or any other nation."[2] "We believe the most important vital sign in the new ecosystems of mainstream Protestantism will be the congregations' ministry with families."[3]

One way to translate that last sentence into an operational system could be to encourage the creation of one or more nongeographical midlevel affinity judicatories composed only of congregations that had decided their top priority is to strengthen, enrich, and expand their ministries with families. A different affinity judicatory could be organized for those congregations that have defined their distinctive missional role as multisite churches. A third affinity judicatory could be created by and for those congregations that have made sheltering the homeless their number-one missional priority. A fourth affinity judicatory could be organized by and for those congregations that have made their top missional priority partnering with indigenous leadership to plant new worshiping communities on other continents.[4] A fifth affinity judicatory could be created by and for those congregations that are convinced God has called them to correct and improve the moral values of the American culture. Several affinity judicatories could be created by and for those congregations that have placed a high priority on ministries with and for that rapidly growing number of one-person households in America.

These are offered as examples of how to translate the warnings being issued by that increasing number of monitoring systems into action plans that could renew the organizational systems of American Protestantism.

This also uses one of the least threatening strategies for initiating planned change from within a tradition-driven organization. This is change by addition, not by subtraction. Those congregations that prefer to be affiliated with a geographically defined regional judicatory would not need to change. Only those congregations that agreed no one approach to ministry fits all congregations, that recognized "doing church" today is more difficult than it was in 1975, that wanted the benefits of peer learning, that wanted to continue and reinforce their denominational affiliation rather than turn to a parachurch or paradenominational agency for resourcing, and that concluded they would be comfortable in an affinity judicatory would choose that alternative.

A Second Lesson

A second lesson is illustrated by the current crisis in the Roman Catholic Church in America. For more than two decades the response of the American leaders to those early warning signs could be summarized by one of these three conclusions.

"Let's not talk about it. Maybe if we don't talk about it, the problem will go away."

"Let's not talk about it until after I've retired because I really don't know what to do about it."

"Let's not talk about it out loud. Let's try to cover it up."

What Will Be the Fallout?

Those who are more comfortable talking about the problems of the Roman Catholic Church in America, rather than the issues confronting their own denomination, may prefer to discuss the probable consequences of the current crisis facing Catholic lead-ers. This is NOT a completely irrelevant topic.

This observer is convinced American Protestants will experi-ence a variety of consequences from this crisis.

1. Opinion polls of American Catholics in 2002 suggested that somewhere between two million and six million disillusioned American Catholics will leave their parish. A conservative esti-mate is at least one-half of them will join a Protestant church. Based on interviews with ex-Catholics who are now active mem-bers of Protestant congregations, this observer's guess is these reli-gious migrants will end up in disproportionately large numbers in (a) new Protestant missions where they can help pioneer the new rather than be expected to perpetuate the old, (b) Latino Pentecostal churches, (c) Protestant congregations in which the laity have a major, if not controlling, voice in selecting the next pastor, (d) numerically growing Protestant churches that enjoy the ministry of a preacher, either live or on videotape, who com-bines relevant content with superb communication skills, (e) congregations served by a female pastor, (f) congregations free of denominational rules, restrictions, and demands, (g) congrega-tions that offer at least one Sunday morning worship service organized around Holy Communion, (h) congregations in which that ex-Catholic's new spouse has a powerful attachment to that denominational tradition, and (i) Episcopal and Anglican parishes.

2. There will be less hesitation in demanding that American civil and criminal laws should apply to all religious institutions and leaders.

3. The public scrutiny of all religious institutions in the United States will become commonplace.

4. Protestant denominations that combine a centralized com-mand and control decision-making process with a hierarchical organizational structure will encounter increased difficulty in earning and retaining the loyalty and support of generations born after 1960.

5. There will be an increased demand for better quality and

more open channels of accountability in both congregational and denominational systems.

6. The demand for a more influential voice for the laity will be strengthened.

7. The role of women in the church will be strengthened and expanded.

8. Persons abusing the power of their office are more likely to be disciplined by church authorities.

9. Investigative reporters will uncover scandals in American Protestantism that would have escaped publicity in the 1980s.

10. It will be more difficult for leaders to cover up the misdeeds or incompetence of parish pastors.

11. The current crisis in the Roman Catholic Church in America affirms a lesson taught by scores of other highly central-ized command-and-control systems organized with a hierarchical system including governments, religious bodies, labor unions, and educational institutions. When a series of disastrous decisions spark a rebellion by the constituents, the officials of that hierar-chy become the first victims. When deposed, few of these ex-leaders are willing to take a job as a greeter at the local WalMart store.

A special report in a pro-business news magazine declared, "Faith in corporate America hasn't been so strained since the early 1900s. . . ."[5] Several Roman Catholic scholars contend the current crisis is the greatest threat to the church since the Protestant Reformation of the sixteenth century. The system of governance in scores of institutions of higher education is being challenged by students, faculty, donors, legislators, and alumni. Three of the mainline American Protestant denominations are confronted by the greatest internal forces for schism since the quarrels over slavery in the midnineteenth century. China's rul-ing Communist Party is under huge pressure to design a strategy that will enable it to survive the pressures to create a market-driven economy while also expanding democratic institutions. Old systems are being challenged all around the world!

12. The differences between the religious traditions in

America that carry a heavy Western European heritage and the "made in America" religious traditions will receive more attention in the years ahead.

13. The doctrine of ascending liability will force at least a few regional judicatories in American Protestantism into bankruptcy or receivership. This already has occurred in Canada.

14. The next few years will bring greater pressure to terminate the ministries of the incompetent as well as those accused of unacceptable behavior.

15. Theological seminaries, both Catholic and Protestant, will be expected to improve their processes for screening candidates for the ministry.

16. The shortage of American-born male priests in the Roman Catholic Church in America will force the leadership to consider alternative ways to increase the supply. Among the alternatives that may be considered are these eight.

a.   Import priests from other continents.

b.   Expand the role of the laity to carry out responsibilities formerly restricted to the clergy.

c.   Encourage the candidacy of a larger number of mature males, most of whom are either widowed or divorced, who were born in the 1940–1960 era and, to use Bob Buford's language, are ready to move "from success to significance."

d.   Improve the processes for recruiting candidates for the priesthood.

e.   Lower the standards for ordination.

f.   Actively encourage ordained Protestant parish ministers to seek ordination as Roman Catholic priests. The focus could be on attracting "the best and the brightest" of Protestant clergy born after 1970. A reasonable goal would be to increase the current stream of three or four a year to three or four a month to perhaps an average of more than one hundred annually.

g.   Terminate the requirement for celibacy. Since this is a practice, not a doctrinal issue, that could be done. If it allows for the reinstatement of priests who were laicized in order to marry, this could provide a quick influx of parish staff. In Chicago, for example, local estimates suggest there are nine resigned Roman

Catholic priests for every ten active priests, and similar ratios are to be found in several other large northern cities.

    h.   Open the door to the ordination of women.

The first four of these eight options already are in place. The fifth is now off-limits. The sixth and seventh could be the most productive. The eighth will depend on the values and goals of the next pope.

While it should not be the top of the agenda, the consequences of the crisis in the Roman Catholic Church deserve the attention of the leaders in American Protestantism. Instead of talking about, "How fortunate we are not to be faced with the problems of our Catholic brothers in Christ," it might be more productive to talk about the fallout from that crisis. How will our constituents respond? What questions will they raise about the outcomes from our ecclesiastical system? Or do you believe American Protestantism is immune to the fallout from this crisis in the Roman Catholic Church?

"It couldn't happen here" and other expressions of denial are normal, natural, and predictable responses to messages that bring bad news. This is especially common when the diagnosis that reveals the system is producing undesired outcomes is not accompanied by an easy-to-fill prescription that guarantees desired outcomes.

A More Constructive Conversation

While it is relatively easy to discuss the outcomes produced by the system in another religious tradition, it will be more constructive to focus on four questions concerning your own denomination. The first question requires defining contemporary reality. What are the outcomes this system has been producing? Does our system include an annual performance review that describes the actual outcomes and also compares them with the desired outcomes?

The second question is more subjective. Are we satisfied with those outcomes? If the answer is "Yes," shift the conversation to professional sports, politics, or what's wrong with today's teenagers.

If, however, you are dissatisfied with the recent and current outcomes, ask the third and fourth questions. What are the outcomes we desire? What changes in the present system will be required to produce these desired outcomes?

The next several paragraphs illustrate one focal point for that first question. What are the recent and current outcomes being produced by the current system?

1. During the 1870–1906 era the mainline Protestant denominations dominated the greatest church-planting boom in American history (see appendix F). During the years of 1880–1899 inclusive, the population of the United States increased by an average of 1.3 million annually. That compares to an average annual increase of 2.7 million during the 1980–1999 period.

During those two decades in the late–nineteenth century a total of more than 67,500 new religious congregations were organized in the United States that were still in existence at the end of 1906 when the "Census of Religious Bodies" was conducted by the United States Bureau of the Census. The hundreds of new missions started in those two decades that failed to survive until 1906 are not included in that count. In addition, 15 percent of the 212,230 congregations in existence in 1906 did not report their date of organization.

That figure of 67,500 averaged out to 3,375 new churches organized every year. That compares with an estimated 4,000 new churches opened each year in America during the last two decades of the twentieth century.

The Methodist Episcopal Church, the largest of the six predecessor bodies of what today is The United Methodist Church, organized an average of 375 new missions annually during those two decades while the Southern Methodists averaged 200 annually. The Southern Baptist Convention averaged 345 a year while the Northern Baptist Convention averaged 125.

The Southern Presbyterians averaged 48, the northern Presbyterians (Presbyterian Church in the United States of America) averaged 120 new churches a year for those two decades, the Cumberland Presbyterian Church averaged 42 new congregations, while the United Presbyterian Church of North America averaged 11 new congregations annually. Roman Catholics averaged 188 a year, the Congregationalists 87 annually, the Disciples of Christ 127 a year, and the Protestant Episcopal Church averaged 54 a year.

The two dozen Lutheran bodies in existence in 1906 organized a combined average of 247 new churches each year during those two decades led by the Evangelical Lutheran Synodical Conference in North America with an average of 69 followed by the General Council of the Lutheran Church in North America with an annual average of 43 new missions that were still in existence in 1906.

Among the black denominations, the National Baptist Convention averaged 430 new churches annually, the African Methodist Episcopal Church averaged 120, the Colored Methodist Episcopal Church averaged 40 new congregations annually, and the African Methodist Episcopal Church Zion averaged 37.

An average of only 20 new independent churches were organized annually during those two decades according to that census, but that was up from an average of three each year for the previous two decades of 1860–1879. An average of 66 new independent churches were organized annually in the 1900–1906 years.

By the time the church-planting boom of the last two decades of the twentieth century had arrived, those seven mainline American Protestant denominations had decided to cut back sharply on new church development.[6] Together they planted a combined total of fewer than 300 new missions in the typical year between 1980 and 2000.

The vacuum created by those decisions has been filled by the Southern Baptist Convention, the Assemblies of God, the

Church of God in Christ, the Mormons, a huge variety of non-denominational congregations including immigrant churches, and an unprecedented increase in Pentecostal and charismatic congregations.

2. In 1965, eight years after the creation of this new denomination, the United Church of Christ (UCC) reported a total of 2,067,000 members scattered among 6,952 congregations. Thirty-five years later in 2000, the UCC reported 1,377,000 members in 5,923 congregations. During that thirty-five year period, the population of the United States grew by 44 percent, while the UCC membership decreased by 33 percent. If that membership total had increased at the same rate as the increase in the American population, the UCC would have reported a total of nearly three million members at the end of the twentieth century, more than double the actual total.

3. In 1968 the two predecessor bodies of the Presbyterian Church (U.S.A.) reported a combined total of 4,299,000 members in 12,676 congregations. During the next thirty-two years (a) the population of the United States increased by almost exactly 40 percent, (b) the membership of the PCUSA decreased by 40 percent, and (c) the number of congregations dropped by 1,500. Most observers of denominational mergers agree that ten plus five is unlikely to equal fifteen and more likely to equal twelve or thirteen, but when ten plus five equals nine, is that a desirable outcome? If the membership growth of these two denominations had kept up with the increase in the American population, the total in 2000 would have been approximately six million, not 2.5 million.

4. At the end of 2000 the Episcopal Church in the United States included 1.8 million members scattered among 7,347 congregations, up from 887,000 in 6,725 congregations in 1906. While the population of the United States more than tripled, the membership of this denomination doubled. The statistical record for 2000, however, made it clear this is NOT a large church denomination. Only 2 percent of all congregations reported an

average worship attendance of more than five hundred in 2000 and only thirty-nine parishes (0.53 percent) reported an average worship attendance of more than 750.

At the other end of this size spectrum, nearly one-half (48.3 percent) reported an average worship attendance of seventy-five or fewer. On the one hand the 2 percent (147 parishes) averaging more than five hundred at worship accounted for 12.7 percent of the worshipers on the typical weekend, while the 48.2 percent (3,544 congregations) averaging seventy-five or fewer at worship accounted for only 15.3 percent.

In a religious culture in America where a disproportionately large number of Protestant churchgoers born after 1960 can be found in very large congregations, do those numbers represent desired outcomes?

5. In 1965 the two predecessor denominations of what in 1968 became The United Methodist Church (UMC) reported a combined membership total of slightly more than eleven million in nearly forty-three thousand congregations. During the next thirty-five years (a) the population of the United States increased by 44 percent, (b) the membership of the UMC decreased by 25 percent, and (c) the number of congregations dropped to 35,469 (compared to a combined total of fifty-seven thousand for the six predecessor denominations in 1906 when the population of the United States was less than one-third of the 2000 total). Ten states reported a decrease of 100,000 or more in membership between 1960 and 2000: Illinois 233,000; Indiana 197,000; New York 192,000; Pennsylvania 181,000; Ohio 176,000; West Virginia 135,000; Michigan 123,000; California 113,000; Iowa 111,000; and Kansas 101,000. It is not a coincidence that seven of those ten states reporting a combined net loss of 1.1 million members constituted the heart of the constituency for the Evangelical United Brethren Church. If the membership growth curve of the UMC had paralleled the population increase of the nation, this denomination would have reported approximately 15.8 million members at the end of the twentieth century, nearly

double the actual figure. The membership of the UMC in 2000 was less than the combined total for the predecessor denominations in 1945. Mergers are not always the most productive path to denominational growth!

An examination of the historical record reveals that between 1972 and 2000 the measurable outcome produced by the United Methodist system included (1) a 20 percent decrease in membership, (2) a 10 percent decrease in the number of congregations, (3) a 5 percent decrease in average worship attendance, (4) a 47 percent decrease in average Sunday school attendance, (5) a pattern in which two-thirds of all congregations averaging fewer than thirty-five at worship experienced a decrease in their average worship attendance and/or either dissolved or merged with another church, (6) despite those thousands of mergers and dissolutions, there was a 12 percent increase in the number of small churches averaging fewer than thirty-five at worship, (7) a pattern in which a majority of congregations reporting an average worship attendance of one hundred or more reported an increase in their average worship attendance, and (8) a 13 percent decrease in the number of congregations reporting an average worship attendance of 100 or more.

In other words, for nearly three decades the UMC system has produced an increase in the number of congregations most likely to shrink in size or to disappear and a sharp decrease in the number of churches most likely to experience numerical growth.

The good news is the number reporting an average worship attendance of 1,001 or more has increased from sixty-five in 1965 to 102 in 2000. The bad news is the number of Protestant congregations in America in that size bracket has at least tripled, perhaps quadrupled since 1965.

It should be added that together those 102 very large UM congregations have accounted for all the net growth in worship attendance in this denomination since 1990.

6. In 1968 the Christian Church (Disciples of Christ) reported 1.6 million members in 5,862 congregations. Thirty-two years later the equivalent numbers were 528,000 members in 3,781

congregations. Part of that decline was more apparent than real as hundreds of congregations chose not to continue their affiliation following the restructure of the mid-1960s that replaced a movement with a denomination. A more useful benchmark may be the reports for the year 1982 that identified 770,000 participating members in 4,328 congregations in the United States and Canada. The average worship attendance (368,600)-to-membership ratio in 1982 was 46 percent compared to 265,282 and a ratio of 32 percent in 2000.

7. In May 1987 the merger of three Lutheran bodies led to the creation of the Evangelical Lutheran Church in America. After "the shakedown cruise" was completed, this new denomination reported 5,245,177 baptized members in 11,074 congregations at the end of 1991. That baptized membership was equal to 2.06 percent of the American population on December 31, 1991. Nine years later the ELCA reported 10,816 congregations with a combined baptized membership of 5,125,919—equal to 1.81 percent of the official population of the United States.

Despite that decrease of 248 in the total number of congregations, between 1991 and 2001 the number of ELCA churches reporting an average worship attendance of fifty or fewer increased by three hundred.

How do those three changes in the number of congregations, the number of baptized members, and the number of small churches compare with the anticipated outcomes back in the early and mid-1980s when the decisions were being made to merge these three Lutheran bodies?

A provocative frame of reference can be used in looking at the Americanization of the immigrant Protestant churchgoers from Western Europe. As they became Americanized and national ancestry became less influential in defining the identity of both individuals and denominations, most of the Lutherans chose the route of denominational mergers. The twentieth-century record includes the mergers of 1917, 1918, 1930, 1962, 1963, and 1987.

These mergers were preceded by a few million funerals, but eventually the great grandchildren of the Scandinavian and German immigrants were able to come together in a new denomination, the Evangelical Lutheran Church in America, that largely depends on the English language to proclaim the gospel of Jesus Christ in America.

A different road was chosen by five other Protestant immigrant religious bodies from Sweden and Germany. As the children and grandchildren became Americanized, instead of promoting denominational mergers, the leaders of the Baptist General Conference (Swedish), the North American Baptist Conference (German), the Evangelical Covenant Church (Swedish), the Evangelical Free Church in America (Swedish), and the Wisconsin Evangelical Lutheran Synod (a product of a 1917 merger of German Lutheran bodies) have focused on (a) preaching and teaching a clearly and precisely defined belief system, (b) evangelism, and (c) missions. Christian unity is not a pressing concern on the contemporary agenda of these five denominations.

It may be only a coincidence, but the ELCA and its predecessor denominations have experienced a numerical decline in recent decades while the other five report numerical growth.

Overcoming Denial

Denial is a natural response to bad news. One component of a strategy for overcoming denial is the capability for constructive self-criticism. A second is to flood the system with accurate, reliable, and relevant information. A third is a willingness to talk openly and constructively about what this means. A fourth is to minimize the time and energy devoted to identifying and blaming a scapegoat. A fifth is to look at the larger context for meaning and direction.

When the fifty-seven-year-old father is told by his doctor he is terminally ill and that is confirmed by second and third opinions from specialists, one temptation is to place the blame on someone else. A second is to be filled with despair. A better option for the Christian is to talk about the Resurrection.

When a Christian congregation or denomination receives what is identified as bad news about the outcomes being produced by the current system, one temptation is denial. A second is to identify a scapegoat. A better option is to talk about how the system can be re-invented to fulfill the Great Commission.

Before doing that, however, it may be productive to talk about what you believe.

CHAPTER THREE

WHAT DO YOU BELIEVE?

Very few denominational policymakers, either paid staff or volunteer, come to the table without any convictions, assumptions, values, hopes, dreams, biases, doctrinal positions, preferences, or other intellectual baggage. It is much easier for a group of individuals to work together to design a ministry plan if they share several assumptions about both contemporary reality and what the future will bring.

If your denominational leaders decide to develop a strategy for ministry in the twenty-first century and to design the organizational structure required to implement that strategy, a useful beginning point could be to seek agreement among the policymakers on the following twenty-four questions.

1. In 1989 Roger Finke and Rodney Stark published a seminal essay that analyzed the "religious economy" of the 1776–1850 era.

They used denominational statistics to explain how the liberal mainline Protestant denominations of that era—Congregationalists, Episcopalians, and Presbyterians—dominated the colonial ecclesiastical scene in the pre-Revolutionary era. In three-quarters of a century, however, ". . . they had slumped into numerical insignificance while the Methodists and Baptists swept over the land."[1]

Their definition of "market share" refers to the proportion of "religious adherents" affiliated with the congregations in that denomination. All six of the religious traditions they cite experienced a sharp growth in membership during that three-quarters of a century, but the market share for the Congregationalists plunged from 20.4 percent in 1776 to 4 percent in 1850; the Episcopalians dropped from 15.7 percent to 3.5 percent; and the Presbyterians experienced a more modest change, shrinking from 19 percent to 11.6 percent. (A contemporary example of "market share" is the state of Utah where The Church of Jesus Christ of Latter-day Saints reports 88 percent of those claiming a religious affiliation identify with that body.)

The "upstarts" included the Baptists who increased their market share from 16.9 percent in 1776 to 20.5 percent in 1850; the Methodists, who expanded their market share from 2.5 percent in 1776 to 34.2 percent in 1850; and the Catholics who grew from 1.8 percent in 1776 to 13.9 percent in 1850.

The central thesis of that essay is those three liberal Protestant bodies that had "been dominated by the privileged and powerful" began to lose their share of the churchgoing market in the last quarter of the nineteenth century, not in the middle of the twentieth. The explanation offered by Finke and Stark was that the religious bodies that gained market share emphasized "otherworldliness" while those that focused on "worldliness" lost in market share.

Finke and Stark added that the greater the degree of clergy control of the denomination, the more likely that religious body would lose market share, while the Methodists and Baptists lifted up the role of the laity and gained market share. In this brief essay, they also point out that the subsequent decline in the

Methodist market share coincided with the professionalization of the Methodist clergy and their demand for an educated clergy.[2]

Between 1940 and 1985 Finke and Stark reported the market share for United Methodists dropped by 48 percent, for the Presbyterian Church (U.S.A.) that decline was 49 percent, and 38 percent for the Episcopal Church.[3]

The Finke-Stark thesis provides a useful conceptual framework for reflecting on the changes in American Christianity during the past half century. While the dollar costs for competing in the American ecclesiastical marketplace have increased sharply since the first half of the nineteenth century, the rising level of affluence has more than offset those increases.

One of the big differences is that the Methodists and the Baptists were the new competitors in the ecclesiastical marketplace two hundred years ago. In recent decades the Bible churches, the Assemblies of God, the Churches of Christ, and the new nondenominational congregations are among those with sharply increasing shares of the religious market.

While the names have changed, the distinction remains the same. During the past half century, it has been what Finke and Stark identified as "the rough and ready upstarts," many without a seminary degree, who launched the new congregations that have attracted the people who prefer a church that places a high value on the role of the laity and emphasizes otherworldliness over worldliness.

This introduces the first of these assumptions and convictions among the policymakers who are charged with designing a strategy for a denominational system. Which of these three scenarios do you believe fits your denomination for the early decades of the twenty-first century?

(a) You believe your denomination can and should achieve an increase in both the number of constituents and also an increase in market share of American churchgoers?

(b) You believe your denomination can and should experience a net gain in the number of constituents but that probably will be accompanied by a loss in market share?

(c) You believe your denomination will experience both a net loss in the number of constituents and a loss in market share.

For example, the six predecessor denominations of today's United Methodist Church included approximately 5.3 million members in 1906 for a market share of 16 percent of the total number of members reported by 212,230 religious congregations in the United States in that year. By the end of 2000 that membership had grown to 8.4 million with a total of 11 million adherents, who represented 7 percent of the estimated 165 million Americans affiliated with a religious congregation in 2000. During that ninety-four year period, the population of the U.S. increased from 85 million to 282 million.

In 1906 all Lutheran churches reported a combined membership of 2.2 million for a market share of 6.7 percent of all reported church members in that year.

All Presbyterian churches reported a combined membership of 1.9 million for a market share of well over 5 percent. In terms of adherents in 2000 the combined market share for all Lutheran bodies was slightly under 5 percent, and the combined market share for all Presbyterian denominations was approximately 2 percent.

It is possible to create self-fulfilling prophecies!

2. The second big question for the policymakers around that table is a recurring theme of this book. Do you believe systems produce the outcomes they are designed to produce? Or do you believe systems are neutral and the key variable is in the values, competence, priorities, policies, goals, dreams, hopes, and biases of the people who staff that system? In other words, if different outcomes are desired, do you focus on changing the system or on replacing the people who staff the system?

3. Do you believe the congregation averaging 350 at worship has more in common with (a) a congregation of the same denomination averaging thirty-five at worship and meeting in a building fifteen miles away or (b) a congregation of the same denomination also averaging 350 at worship, meeting in a similar building located in a similar community setting, but in another state?

Do you believe old First Church downtown averaging three hundred at worship, down from six hundred in 1955, but up from 155 in 1975, has more in common with (a) a congregation of the same denomination averaging thirty-five at worship and meeting in a building seven miles away or (b) a new suburban mission of the same denomination now averaging five hundred at worship in its third year of existence and meeting in a public school six miles to the west or (c) another Old First Church downtown meeting in a similar size city four hundred miles away?

Do you believe geographical proximity or institutional commonality is the more important variable as congregational leaders seek to benefit from the learnings of leaders in other congregations?

During the nineteenth and early twentieth centuries in America the geographically defined neighborhood began to replace the clan as the basic unit beyond the family in building social systems. The central organizing principle of the clan was kinship ties and/or language and/or ancestry and/or religious affiliation and/or skin color and/or social class and/or occupation and/or military service. Neighborhoods tended to be organized around the geographical proximity of the place of residence and/or institutions such as schools, churches, retail stores, post offices, and/or cooperation in making a living or in rearing children.

What do you believe will be the most common central organizing principle as Americans in 2010 build their personal social networks? Will it be kinshp ties? Or place of work? Or shared experiences in recreation and hobbies? Or profession? Or military service? Or church affiliation? Or nationality, ancestry, language, and/or skin color? Or education? Or the geographical proximity of the place of residence? Or age? Or stage of the life cycle? Or health? Or financial resources?

4. Do you believe most of the babies born in the United States between 1980–2000 will inherit their religious affiliation from their parents? Or do you believe they will choose their own religious affiliation? Or choose the church closest to their place of residence?

5. Do you believe the journey to work, the journey from home to retail shopping, the journey to recreational activities and events, the journey to healthcare facilities, and the journey to church will be (a) longer in 2010 than it was in 1960 or (b) shorter than it was in 1960?

6. Do you believe the number-one source of creativity, wisdom, and knowledge on how to carry out effective, relevant, and high quality ministries in 2010 will be (a) theological seminaries, (b) Bible colleges, (c) national denominational headquarters, (d) parachurch organizations, (e) retreat centers, (f) regional denominational judicatories, (g) self-identified teaching churches, or (h) congregations founded after 2000?

Pick the one you believe will most likely reflect contemporary reality in 2010. Does that choice differ from what you believe was contemporary reality in 1960? Does your choice differ from what you prefer would be contemporary reality in 2010?

7. Do you believe it is easier for a pastor (a) to revitalize a long-established congregation with an aging and numerically shrinking constituency or (b) to lead a team of three-to-five full-time specialists in ministry who will plant a new mission that will average three hundred or more at worship within three years after the first public worship service is held?

8. What do you believe is the minimum size for a congregation to both challenge the creativity and energy of a full-time and fully credentialed resident pastor and also be economically viable? (a) an average worship attendance of sixty or more, (b) an average worship attendance of eighty-five to 100 or more, (c) an average worship attendance of 100 to 120 or more, (d) an average worship attendance of at least 135?

9. As a congregation seeks a successor for the departing pastor, do you believe it is no more difficult today than it was in 1960 to find the ideal match between the gifts, skills, theological stance, personality, experience, work ethic, priorities, and family status of a pastor and the needs of that particular church? Or do you believe it is more difficult today to find that ideal match?

If you believe it is more difficult today, does that lead you to conclude the time has come to replace the traditional regional marketplace for ministers with a national marketplace?

10. What do you believe should be the ideal minimum length of a pastorate for a minister serving a congregation currently averaging 350 or more at worship? (This question assumes that two ordained ministers will serve the congregation, and the question refers to the tenure of the senior pastor.) (a) five to seven years? (b) seven to ten years? (c) ten to fifteen years? (d) More than sixteen years?

THE 33RD PERCENTILE

One-Third of All Congregations Averaged This Number or Fewer at Worship in 1999

United Methodist	36
Presbyterian (PCUSA)	48
Assemblies of God	48
Episcopal Church	50
Disciples of Christ	53
Southern Baptist Convention	54
Evangelical Lutheran Church in America	71
Baptist General Conference	73
Evangelical Free Church	85

11. In most of the mainline Protestant denominations, one-third or more of their affiliated congregations report an average worship attendance of fifty-five or fewer. What do you believe is the best way to provide ministerial leadership for these small congregations?

(a) Part-time trained lay ministers?

(b) A financial subsidy from the denomination to enable each congregation to benefit from the leadership of a full-time and seminary-trained resident pastor?

(c) Part-time pastors concurrently enrolled in college or seminary?

(d) Share a full-time and fully credentialed pastor with another congregation of the same denomination?

(e)   Share a full-time and fully credentialed pastor with another congregation of a different denomination?

(f)   Share a full-time and fully credentialed pastor with two or more other congregations?

(g)   Share a part-time student pastor with two or more small churches?

(h)   Share the leadership of a clergy couple with two or more congregations?

(i)   Share the leadership of a ministerial team serving several small churches?

(j)   Develop its own indigenous leadership from among its own constituents?

(k)   Request the leadership of a three-person trained lay team who are members of a large church that specializes in enlisting, training, placing, nurturing, and supporting lay volunteer teams to serve small churches?

(l)   Rely on part-time semiretired ordained ministers?

(m)   Turn to ordained ministers with a seminary degree who are serving in full-time positions (teaching, chaplaincy, etc.) that does not require them to work Sundays who desire to serve as part-time pastors?

(n)   Call the spouse who is a seminary graduate and wants to combine the roles of a part-time pastor and a part-time home-maker while the other spouse is the primary breadwinner for that family or

(o)   Rely on the "bottom of the barrel" among the pastors in the ministerial marketplace?

12. Do you believe the future of American Protestantism is with the small congregation? Or the midsize church averaging between one hundred and seven hundred at worship? Or with the very large congregations averaging more than eight hundred at worship?

During the twentieth century the average (mean) size of congregations in American Protestantism tripled. Do you believe that represents part of a larger long-term trend? Or will the twenty-first century bring a return to smaller institutions including smaller churches?

For example, between 1972 and 2000 The United Methodist Church, through mergers and dissolutions, eliminated at least a thousand very small congregations. During that twenty-eight year period, however, the number of United Methodist congregations reporting an average worship attendance of fewer than thirty-five increased by a thousand while those reporting an average worship attendance of thirty-five or more decreased by more than 3,600.

A second example is the Presbyterian Church (U.S.A.). A total of 1,910 PCUSA congregations reported an average worship attendance of thirty or fewer for 1999, up from 1,779 in 1990, while the number reporting an average worship attendance of more than thirty decreased by approximately five hundred.

As you develop a strategy for your denomination for the twenty-first century and design an organizational structure for implementing that structure, do you believe that plan should be designed to (a) increase or (b) decrease the number of congregations averaging fewer than thirty-five at worship? Or should it be designed to increase the proportion that average at least 350 at worship?

13. At the end of the twentieth century, the largest 1 percent of the congregations in an American Protestant denomination accounted for somewhere between 8 and 15 percent of all the people worshiping with churches affiliated with that denomination during the typical week.

WHERE DO PEOPLE GO TO CHURCH?

The Largest 40 Percent of Congregations Account for What Proportion of Worshipers?

Ev. Luth. Ch. Am.	75%
Evangelical Covenant	76%
Episcopal	76%
UMC	78%
Assemblies of God	80%
Evangelical Presbyterian	83%

In most Protestant denominations that ask congregations to report their average worship attendance, these reports reveal that the largest 40 percent of all congregations affiliated with that denomination account for somewhere between 73 percent and 85 percent of all worshipers on the typical weekend while the other 60 percent account for 15 to 27 percent.

What proportion of the congregations in your denomination will account for three-quarters of the people worshiping with a church of your denomination in 2010? Do you believe 25 percent will account for three-quarters of those worshipers? Or 30 percent? Or 40 percent? Or 50 percent?

One of the most significant trends of recent years is the increase in the number of larger congregations that have decided to become multisite ministries. They continue with one message, one name, one governing board, one staff, one budget, one treasury, and one image, but with two or more meeting places. Most limit themselves to two or three separate locations, but a few minister from somewhere between five and two hundred sites. Many choose this option instead of sponsoring new missions. Others choose it instead of relocating from their current meeting place.

Do you believe your denomination should (a) encourage congregations to give serious consideration to this option or (b) discourage that choice?

14. What do you believe is the minimum size for a viable congregation in contemporary American Protestantism?

An answer, of course, depends on the definition of that word "viable." Despite the statement by Jesus, "For where two or three are gathered in my name, I am there among them" (Matthew 18:20); a reasonable beginning point for defining the minimum size of a continuing worshiping community could evoke the question, "What happens if two or three of those regular worshipers are out of town or ill or incapacitated for several weeks?" A reasonable response is if that worshiping community averages seven or eight at worship, it continues to be viable when two or three are absent. (In 2000 and 2001 a total of 439 United Methodist, 130 Southern Baptist, 58 Assemblies of God, 54 PCUSA, and 14

ELCA congregations reported an average worship attendance of either seven or eight.)

A second part of the answer is revealed by the fact that the five most frequently reported numbers for average worship attendance in several American Protestant denominations are 20, 25, 30, 35, and 40.

Therefore, it seems reasonable to suggest an average worship attendance of seven to forty could be identified as viable. That definition may be offensive to some readers because it suggests the 59 Assemblies of God, 61 Presbyterian (U.S.A.), 80 Southern Baptist, 16 ELCA, and 373 United Methodist congregations reporting a worship attendance of six or fewer at the end of the twentieth century are not viable. That, however, is not a battle we will fight here.

That broad definition of an average worship attendance of seven to forty includes an estimated 25,000 nondenominational and mostly lay-led Protestant house churches, more than 3,000 Assemblies of God, more than 8,000 Southern Baptist, more than 1,600 ELCA, more than 2,600 Presbyterian (U.S.A.), and more than 13,000 United Methodist congregations. A few are served by a full-time pastor, others share a minister with another congregation, while most are lay-led.

A completely different definition of viability calls for a congregation to be able to afford, attract, challenge, and retain the services of a full-time, fully credentialed, seminary-trained, and resident pastor. That usually means an average worship attendance of 125 or more. Fewer than three out of ten American Protestant churches reach that standard of viability.

American churchgoers born after 1960 tend to project higher expectations of person-centered institutions (public schools, hospitals, local government, churches, grocery stores, pharmacies, financial institutions) than were projected by their parents and grandparents. Many look for the "full-service bank." They prefer the supermarket that also houses a pharmacy, a coffee shop, a branch bank, a place to purchase flowers, magazines, and greeting cards, and ready-to-heat-and-serve food. Their definition of a full-service church may include two worship services on Sunday morning, plus one or two Saturday evening worship experiences, a full scale Sunday school, an attractive youth ministry, and an extensive package of Monday-to-Saturday ministries.

Which congregations can mobilize the resources required to be a full-service church if that is the definition of viability? Experience suggests an average worship attendance of 300 to 350 or more. If that level of viability is defined as more than 300 at worship, that short list excludes 83 percent to 93 percent of all the congregations in the larger denominations in contemporary American Protestantism.

The increasing competition among congregations for new members also has created another definition of viability called "being competitive." The most highly visible and measurable indicator of this new definition is reported by those American Protestant congregations that report one-third to three-fourths of their adult new constituents as people who migrated to their church from a Roman Catholic heritage or from a different Protestant affiliation. The contemporary American economy is far more competitive than it was in the 1970s. That generalization applies to selling groceries, medicines, hogs, newspapers, gasoline, a seat on a commercial airliner, motor vehicles, wheat, office supplies, magazines, and soft drinks. It also applies to the quest by Protestant congregations for future constituents.

Another indicator of viability is what proportion of those first-time visitors who are shopping for a new church home return the following week.

The competitive churches report more than one-half of those first-time visitors who are church shopping choose this as their permanent church home. Year after year they report an increase in their average worship attendance. For most of them, baptisms exceed constituent deaths by a three-to-one or greater ratio.

For denominationally affiliated congregations, another yardstick for evaluating viability is the proportion of newcomers to that community who have left behind affiliation with a congregation of that denomination and choose a new church home by an intradenominational transfer.

How large does a contemporary American Protestant

congregation need to be to be competitive? In rural America the answer may be 125 at worship. In many large central cities the answer may be an average of three hundred at worship. In the numerically growing cities and suburban communities, the answer usually is at least eight hundred at worship.

As you plan for the future of your denomination, what is your definition of a "viable congregation"?

15. That discussion introduces another question. What do you believe is the minimum size for a new mission to be both viable and competitive?

The vast majority of new missions launched by the mainline Protestant denominations in the second half of the twentieth century were designed to be small churches. That design usually included (a) planting a new mission to serve a geographically defined constituency, (b) sending a solo pastor, rather than a team, to organize that new church, (c) purchasing a site of less than five acres as the future permanent meeting place, (d) using an elementary school building as the temporary meeting place, (e) scheduling that crucial first public worship service for an attendance of fewer than three hundred, thus attracting adults who prefer the intimacy of a small single-cell fellowship, (f) choosing a mission-developer pastor who had never served on the staff of a very large congregation and therefore was comfortable with the culture and dynamics of the small church, (g) providing a three-year or longer operational subsidy, thus undermining the goal of quickly becoming a self-expressing, self-governing, self-financing, and self-propagating congregation, and (h) the assumption that mission-developer pastor would serve that congregation for fewer than twenty years.

Those committed to that design could point to the success stories in which a particular new mission was averaging more than five hundred at worship by the end of the fifth year as evidence that design was sound. The reason offered for the fact that only one in ten new missions matched that growth curve was the incompetence of the mission-developer pastor. Why did that aircraft crash? Was it pilot error or a design flaw?

As you plan for the role of your denomination in the

twenty-first century, do you believe new missions should be designed to plateau with an average worship attendance of fewer than 150? Or to close before the tenth birthday? Or to exceed an average worship attendance of five hundred by the end of the fifth year?

Or do you believe the design is irrelevant and the crucial variable is choosing the right mission-developer pastor?

16. For a variety of reasons, it appears the number of "cradle Catholics" leaving the Roman Catholic Church in America will continue to increase during the early years of the twenty-first century. (See chapter 2.) Most of these religious migrants were born after 1950 and a disproportionately large number are parents with children at home.

Do you believe the congregations affiliated with your denomination should open their doors wide to welcome these people on their personal faith pilgrimage? Or do you believe your congregations should concentrate on reaching and converting nonbelievers? Or do you believe that an affirmation of ecumenism means your congregations should discourage Catholics on a self-identified search for a new church home from joining one of your congregations?

17. The number of Americans of all ages who both live and work on farms has plunged from thirty-two million in 1920 to twenty-seven million in 1947 to approximately two million in 2002. The redefinition of what formerly were classified as rural counties in the United States into metropolitan areas has meant the rural population of the nation has remained relatively constant at between fifty and fifty-five million since 1940—but that fifty-five million in 2000 was concentrated in far fewer counties than the fifty million of 1940.

Do you believe these demographic trends mean a severely limited future for rural farming congregations? Or do you believe these trends open the door to substantial numerical growth for your denomination in rural America?

In 1999 the fifth largest congregation in The United Methodist Church, using average worship attendance to measure size, worshiped in a building in the open country in rural Ohio. With an average worship attendance of 3,012 for the year, it stands out as one of the largest open country churches in America. Do you believe that is an aberration? Or should it be viewed as a model of what can happen in the twenty-first century?

18. For several generations American Christians enlisted fellow Christians to go to other continents to win converts to Jesus Christ and to organize new worshiping communities. One consequence of success came when the career American missionaries began to enlist and equip indigenous leaders to pioneer the creation of new Christian churches on other continents. Both of these strategies usually were financed by dollars collected in American churches and channeled through a denominational foreign missionary agency. (In the *World Christian Encyclopedia* Michael Jeffarian reports the United States currently sends 118,000 missionaries to other lands, substantially more than the combined total of 93,000 sent by Italy, France, and Spain, the next three on the list of missionary-sending nations. Jaffarian also reports the United States leads the world as a destination for missionaries with 33,200 followed by Brazil, Russia, and France.)

More recently American parachurch and paradenominational agencies have been raising the money, enlisting and equipping missionaries, and planting new Christian churches on other continents. During the past several years a growing number of American Protestant congregations have accepted the direct responsibility to plant what have become sister churches in Latin America, Africa, Asia, and Eastern Europe. This fourth strategy usually includes enlisting short-term American missionaries as well as indigenous leaders to implement that call to plant new missions.

Which of these four strategies do you believe should be the norm for your denomination in the twenty-first century?

19. For most of the history of American Protestantism, new congregations in this country were the creation either of existing congregations or of a group of believers, often recent immigrants, who accepted the initiative to organize a new worshiping community. The nineteenth century brought a new player into this game as denominational leaders and missionary societies accepted the responsibility to be initiating leaders in new church

development. During the second half of the twentieth century an increasing proportion of new Protestant congregations were created by existing churches, by entrepreneurial clergy, by immigrant clergy, by small groups of laity, by Christian missionaries to the United States from other continents, and by informal partnerships of two to ten existing churches.

What do you believe should be the two core components of your denomination's strategy for new church development in the twenty-first century?

20. What do you believe should be the three core components of your denomination's strategy for preparing the next generation of clergy and paid lay staff for congregations in the twenty-first century? Should those three include (a) residential Bible colleges, (b) residential professional schools such as theological seminaries, (c) residential graduate schools such as university divinity schools or schools of religion, (d) postseminary apprenticeships of three to seven years on the staff of very large churches, (e) one- or two-year internships on the staff of a teaching church between the second and third year of seminary education, (f) a postseminary apprenticeship of three to twenty years serving as the pastor of small congregations, (g) focusing primarily on Christians, age forty-five and over, who are ready for a new career, (h) a continuing role on the program staff of a self-identified teaching church concurrently with classroom instruction on that congregation's campus in the academic courses required for an academic degree, (i) a partnership between a teaching church and a theological seminary with all classroom instruction on the campus of that teaching church, (j) challenging lay volunteers who are fully devoted followers of Jesus Christ to combine a role as a paid staff member with on-the-job training experiences as preparation for a new career in the parish ministry, (k) distance learning, or (l) some other option?

21. Do you believe one of the central responsibilities of your denominational system is to take better care of pastors in the twenty-first century than was the practice in the twentieth century?

That list of responsibilities may include equitable compensation, placement, health insurance, counseling, pensions, better
housing, vocational promotions, continuing education, spiritual
mentoring, legal defense in case of litigation, job security, and
early retirement.

22. The Western European institutional expression of
Christianity was largely a clergy-centered and clergy-driven
model. Most of the "made-in-America" Christian traditions
have, at least in their early decades, placed a far greater emphasis
on the role of the laity.

Do you believe the organizational structure for your denomination for the twenty-first century should (a) expand the role,
responsibility, and authority of the laity or (b) be a clergy-driven
model? Do you believe that one of the primary reasons for the
existence of a denominational system is to regulate the beliefs,
behavior, practices, and ideology of congregations and local leaders?

23. If forced to make a choice between (a) organizing new
congregations to win new generations of American-born residents and recent immigrants to Christ and enhancing the effectiveness of existing churches or (b) promoting Christian unity,
which do you believe should be the driving force in designing an
organizational structure for your denomination in the twenty-
first century? (If your denomination is the only one to adopt the
concept of nongeographical affinity judicatories and/or that
action reduces the authority vested in the national offices of your
denomination that could be a barrier to increased interdenominational cooperation.)

24. From the early years of the seventeenth century through
the first several decades of the twentieth century, the religious
culture of America reflected evangelical Protestant ideology and
practices. Alan Wolfe contends the dominant attitude among
Americans today on religious matters is tolerance.[4] More recently
the change in immigration patterns has expanded the participants in interfaith conversations from the traditional three parties of the 1960s to four or five or six or seven.

Do you believe this will mean John 14:6 will be a more influential or a less influential line of demarcation in twenty-first-century America?

What Do You Bring to the Table?

In the ideal world when the policymakers come to the table to design a strategy for your denomination for the twenty-first century, they will be able to focus on a single question. What are the outcomes the Lord expects our denominational system to produce? (See chapter 6.) A subsequent question should be what is the organizational system most likely to produce those outcomes?

This chapter is placed early in this book on the conviction that process will be facilitated if those policymakers share a common perspective in terms of assumptions, values, dreams, goals, preferences, and ideology. That process also will be facilitated if those policymakers share a common understanding of contemporary reality. That explains why the next chapter focuses on how affluence has changed contemporary reality in America.

CHAPTER FOUR

WHAT ARE THE CONSEQUENCES OF AFFLUENCE?

For most of human history the daily schedule for the overwhelming majority of adults was organized around personal survival goals and the rearing of offspring. That generalization still applies to millions of residents of the Third World, as well as to birds, squirrels, rabbits, and millions of human beings in North America. Once upon a time, children, if they were fortunate, could hope their life as adults would be as good as life was for their parents. Today many children all over this planet expect life should be better for them than it has been for their parents. Millions are convinced the road to achieving that dream is to migrate to the United States.

The Demand for the Good Life

What is the good life? Once upon a time it was the life enjoyed by the more fortunate of your relatives, neighbors, and nearby friends. A century or two ago a small proportion of the world's children began to learn about the good life of others as they attended school, learned to read, and thus discovered how people lived in other parts of this world. In the middle third of the twentieth century motion pictures came along to teach both children and adults about other definitions of the good life. During the past few decades, television has supplemented printed resources and motion pictures in describing the good life to children all around the world.

This demand for the right to the good life is one of a dozen consequences of affluence to be discussed in this chapter. Like every cultural, societal, and economic change, however, it comes with a price tag.

For several years the Taliban in Afghanistan recognized the power of the printed word, of motion pictures, and of television. All three channels of communication fed the fires of discontent with the authorities' definition of the good life. The solution was to ban motion pictures and television. Girls were prohibited from going to school, and education for boys focused on memorizing the Koran. The right to the good life can and often does encounter opposition.

Education, motion pictures, and television are among the consequences of affluence. Together they communicate the message that a better life is not simply a hope or a dream, it is a right. That revolutionary document Americans call the Declaration of Independence articulated that right. The right to a better life for oneself and for one's children may be the most significant single consequence of affluence.

The Right of Self-determination

One component of a better life is the right to have greater control over one's own personal future. The replacement of the military draft with volunteer military organizations was one of scores of recent American affirmations of this right of self-determination. The increased reliance on referenda and voter initiatives in those states that allow these expressions of participatory democracy represent another form of self-determination. The use of presidential primaries every four years to choose candidates for the presidency of the United States instead of granting that power to party conventions, is another. The rapid increase in the number of nondenominational Protestant churches and the decrease in the number affiliated with an episcopal system of governance represents another consequence of affluence and the demand for self-determination.

One of the more interesting expressions of self-determination is reflected in the names American parents give to their newborn children. A common custom among generations of Americans was to name that new baby after an older member of the family tree. Anne, Barbara, David, Edward, Elizabeth, Frank, Frederick, Helen, James, Joseph, Katherine, Mary, Nancy, Paul, Ruth, Susan, Theodore, Thomas, and William were among the most common first names in the United States through the 1960s. Among the twenty most frequently used names given to girls and the twenty for boys born in the United States in 2001, only Elizabeth, Joseph, William, David, John, and James were among the most popular names of the first seven decades of the twentieth century and also were on either of the two lists for the twenty most popular names for babies born in 2001. (Emily, Madison, Hannah, Jacob, Michael, and Matthew topped the two lists for babies born in 2001.)

Self-determination and individualism have moved ahead of kinship ties and tradition as influential factors in decision making among the generations born after 1960.

The Battle over Regulation

Once upon a time the American culture taught everyone that younger generations needed not only the advice and counsel of their elders, but also a carefully structured regulatory environment if they were to enjoy the good life as adults. As life became more complicated, the cry for more regulation became louder. That trend has been expressed in agriculture, the work place, the stock market, transportation, communication systems, entertainment, education, the delivery of health care services, housing, and professional sports.

A natural expression of that assumption also motivated several Christian bodies, including the Roman Catholic Church, to accept the responsibility for expanding their regulatory role over both the clergy and congregational life. The more this regulatory role for religious systems grew, the more obvious it became to the regulators that even more regulation was needed. That trend is a natural, normal, and predictable tendency in every regulatory body.

Regulation costs money. In an economic system organized around a scarcity of resources that limited the expansion of regulatory bodies. Who should pay the costs of being regulated? The obvious answer was those being regulated.

The last several years have brought a conflict between that right of self-determination and the culture of regulation. On the world scene the Taliban came into power in Afghanistan as a regulatory force. When they were defeated, the right of self-determination brought a sharp increase in crime. The demand for self-determination produced the end of the Union of Soviet Socialist Republics in the late 1980s. It has also terminated the rule of several dictatorships on the world scene, often followed by severe economic disruptions. Every major change produces unanticipated consequences.

In the American economy this conflict between regulation and control and the right of self-determination has produced political battles over land use controls, the consumption of gasoline in motor vehicles, the design of systems for providing health care, free agency and owner-player negotiations in major league baseball, the production and distribution of electricity and gasoline, the values to drive the distribution of federal financial subsidies to agriculture, the consumption of alcoholic beverages by teenage undergraduates on college and university campuses, and dress codes in the public schools.

One of the most divisive consequences on the American ecclesiastical scene of this conflict between the growing demand for self-determination and regulatory authorities can be seen in the competition for the charitable dollar. Who should control the final destination of those dollars dropped in the offering plate during Sunday morning worship? The donor through designated contributions? The finance committee in that congregation? The officials of the regional judicatory? The officials of national denominational agencies?[1]

The number of charitable dollars contributed by individuals and families has increased sharply since the early 1990s. The proportion flowing through congregational and denominational channels has decreased, however, as the donors chose to send those dollars directly to their favorite cause.

An interesting example of this conflict between self-determination and regulation made national news in the winter of 2002. The archbishop of the Los Angeles Diocese of the Roman Catholic Church removed twelve priests from active duty because of allegations of sexual abuse of children and youth. Across the continent the bishop of the Diocese of Maine responded to confessions by two Roman Catholic priests that they had been guilty of pedophilia. Instead of removing them from their assignments, he declared that in each case the local parish council should exercise its right of self-determination by recommending whether their priest should continue to serve that parish or be removed.[2]

Delayed Entrance and Earlier Exit

One of the most significant American consequences of affluence has been in postponing a person's entrance into the labor
force. One early manifestation of this created the demand for tax-
supported public high schools. What should we do with fourteen-
year-olds? The traditional response had been, "Put them to
work!" The urbanization of America and the rise of affluence following the Civil War undermined that simple solution, and child
labor laws became more common. The new solution was to ware-
house them for a couple of years in public high schools.[3]

By the 1930s the Great Depression created a new problem.
What should we do with that record crop of babies born after
World War I? What should we do with all those eighteen-year-
olds? One solution was creation of the Civilian Conservation
Corps. In 1943 a new alternative was created when the age for
the military draft was lowered to eighteen.

The affluent American economy of the post–World War II era
created another solution. Send those teenagers to college! In
1950 one out of every three Americans, age twenty-five and over,
had completed four years of high school. Fifty years later that proportion was six out of seven. In 1950 only 6 percent of American
residents, age twenty-five and over, had completed four or more
years of college. By 2000 that proportion had quadruped to 25
percent.

Sooner or later nearly every parent discovers education is
alienating. All over this planet education has alienated younger
generations from local and national traditions, from being content with the status quo, and from the control of those in positions of authority. In the United States education, and especially
higher education, has alienated huge numbers of young adults
from the religious traditions of their parents.[4]

For most of human history adults worked as long as they were
physically able to do so. In recent decades the Western world
invented the concept of retirement from the labor force. By the
1940s, except for career military personnel, police officers,

firefighters, and pilots of commercial aircraft, age sixty-five was seen as the normal age for retirement. Today one-half of all American males retire before their sixty-second birthday, and many retire earlier. The right to an early and financially secure retirement has been added to that lengthening list of rights created by affluence.

This has more complicated consequences than first appears because of increased life expectancy. A growing number of Americans do not enter the paid labor market until they are in their early twenties. If they retire thirty-five years later, they may spend another quarter century in retirement. The person born in 1880 may have spent fifty-five of his seventy-year life span working. The person born in 1940 may spend only thirty-five years of an eighty-year life span in the labor force.

From a public policy perspective one of the financial consequences of this earlier exit from the labor force is being felt in those organizations that created a defined benefit pension system that never was fully funded. That long list includes many local, state, and federal government pension systems. Future taxpayers are expected to cover that expression of deficit financing. Most Protestant denominations in America now operate with a defined contribution pension system, but many of the orders and dioceses in the Roman Catholic Church in America have not fully funded their pension systems.

One consequence of these changes in the American labor force is the congregations that once assumed nearly every adult parishioner was either employed or a full-time homemaker now serves an adult constituency, one-half of whom are retirees. Another is the availability of physically healthy, mentally alert, and religiously committed adults in their fifties and sixties who can be challenged to launch a new career as a part-time or full-time program staff member of a large church or as the pastor of a small congregation. Earlier retirement has provided the churches with a huge new source of lay ministers, both paid and volunteer.

A third consequence is much remains to be learned about ministry with persons in the eighteen to twenty-eight age bracket who are not in the active labor force, not married, and not parents. We do know most do not want to be classified by their marital status.

A fourth consequence, of course, is that increasing proportion of parish pastors who have decided to take early retirement and/or pursue one more career before their final retirement. The parish ministry no longer is perceived to be a lifetime career.

A fifth consequence is a product of several factors including affluence and changes in the labor market. This also is a change that has been largely overlooked by observers of congregational life and runs contrary to contemporary conventional wisdom. It can best be described by using a hundred-year time frame.

During the first decade of the twentieth century, white males constituted slightly more than 51 percent of the white population of the United States, age fourteen and over. Negro women outnumbered Negro men in the census reports of 1900 and 1910 by a tiny margin that was less than a 51 to 49 ratio. One explanation for those ratios was recent white male immigrants outnumbered recent white female immigrants. A second was the relatively large number of women who died in childbirth.

MALE-FEMALE RATIOS
CHURCH MEMBERSHIP 1906

Lutherans (all)	46-54
Baptists (all)	38-62
Congregationalists	34-66
Methodists (all)	39-61
Presbyterians (all)	38-62
Episcopalians	43-57
Disciples of Christ	40-60
Friends (all)	46-54
Ref. Church in Am.	38-62
Christian Scientist	28-72
Southern Baptists	41-39
Seventh-day Adventists	37-63
Latter-day Saints	49-51
Roman Catholic	49-51

The Census of Religious Bodies of 1906, however, revealed that for all American Protestant congregations female members outnumbered men by a 60.7-to-39.3 ratio—a sharp contrast to the distribution of the American population, age fourteen and over.

The census of population of 2000 reported that American females, age fourteen and over, outnumbered males in that same age cohort by a 52-to-48 ratio. That old turn-of-the-century ratio has been reversed.

What happened to that male-female ratio in the churches? We lack a comprehensive and reliable database. A few denominations do report survey data. The Presbyterian Church (U.S.A.) reported that for 1995 the male-female ratio of members was 46 to 54, and in 1998 it was 41 to 59. That big change probably was due to differences in methodology. During the past forty-plus years we have asked more than a thousand congregations, both denominationally affiliated and independent, to conduct a four-week survey of worship attendance as part of their advance preparation for a parish consultation. Most of the reporting congregations report (1) women tend to attend more frequently than men and (2) on a typical weekend women outnumber men in worship by a 54-to-46 ratio.

During the past hundred years men have gone from a majority to a minority of the American population while their presence in worship is greater today than was their presence on membership rolls in 1906.

The obvious explanation is that in 1906 the vast majority of adult males worked a sixty-to-ninety hour work week, and that left less time for discretionary activities such as reading, travel, vacations, church, sports, or schooling. Perhaps more influential was the American culture of 1900 that emphasized women's threefold responsibilities of kitchen, children, and church. Church was for women and children, not busy men.

One piece of the oral tradition explains that in the late nineteenth century and early twentieth century, American males were more concerned about "running the church" and if they couldn't run it, they were comfortable staying away.

In recent years the opportunities for women in the American labor force have increased. Is that expanded presence of men in the church at least partly a result of the growth in the competition for the discretionary time of women? Is that one reason behind the shrinking number of younger women who are active members of the women's organization in their church? Is the recent rapid increase in the number of men engaged in weekly all-male Bible study and prayer groups a part of this larger trend of a larger presence of adult males in the church? Is this a product of affluence or a national religious revival? Or is it a product of egalitarianism? Or of changes in the American economy and labor market? Or simply new generations bringing new expectations?

Expectations Have Been Raised

Affluence, education, television, advertising, and travel have combined to raise the level of expectations people bring to the table. This consequence can be seen in action when Americans shop for motor vehicles, airline tickets, shoes, groceries, a mortgage on the home they are about to buy, a motel room, coffee, clothes, a new house, a camera, a school for their children, an assisted-living center for that aging parent, a computer, or a church home. They expect high quality, relevance, choices, and an emphasis on customer service. The bar has been raised on what is deemed to be acceptable.[5]

One consequence is an increased demand for relevant continuing education experiences for pastors. Another is the growing proportion of younger churchgoers who, while they do not yearn to be part of a megachurch filled with anonymity and complexity, choose a very large congregation because it is able to mobilize the resources required to fulfill their expectations in terms of quality, relevance, and choices. The weekend schedule may include five or six different worship experiences in three different venues.

A second, and perhaps the most subtle consequence of higher expectations is the erosion of institutional loyalties. World War II reinforced a long history of loyalty by Americans to institutions. That mile-long list included patriotism, an inherited religious allegiance, kinship ties, partisan political allegiance, pride in ancestry, membership in lodges, clubs, veterans' organizations and parent-teacher associations, the loyalty by alumni to the school from which they had graduated, loyalty to employers, family doctors, next door neighbors, and loyalty to their inherited religious tradition. This trend also helps to explain the increase in the number of believers who have "dropped out" of church.

A combination of the civil rights movement and dozens of other protest movements of the 1960s, the rise of individualism, education (which tends to alienate students from their old institutional loyalties), affluence, an increase in upward social mobility, and other factors have produced a substantial number of adult Americans who do not express strong loyalties to institutions. For some their primary loyalty is to themselves. For many others, however, their basic loyalty is to a cause, not an institution.

The big recent national event that illustrated this distinction came in the fall of 2001. Tens of thousands of people made generous contributions to the variety of funds dedicated to the relief of the victims of 9-11-01. The lesson is clear. It is much easier to raise money for a cause than to underwrite the budget required to perpetuate an existing institution.

Here Come the Switchers!

A related consequence is the affluent, well-educated, and dissatisfied customer born after 1940 finds it relatively easy to switch institutional loyalties. One example of that is the shrinking market share of motor vehicle sales experienced by the big three of General Motors, Ford, and Chrysler-Daimler. A second is in the sale of groceries. A third is in airline travel. A fourth is in church affiliation. The recent exodus of "cradle Catholics" to Protestant churches and of members reared in a denominationally affiliated

Protestant church to a new nondenominational mission are two examples.

The American Religious Identification Survey of 2001 reported 8 percent of the Catholic respondents had switched to that faith from a different religious tie, but twice that proportion were ex-Catholics who had switched from Catholicism to another religion. About the same proportion had switched to a Baptist church (13 percent) as had switched from Baptist church. Lutherans (18 percent switched to and 19 percent switched from) and Presbyterians (24 percent to and 25 percent from) also broke even on this pattern of interchurch migration. Of those who were or had been Methodist, 19 percent switched to one of the Methodist denominations while 25 percent left.

The most startling pattern was among those with a former or current nondenominational church affiliation. A remarkable 29 percent had switched to a nondenominational congregation but only 2 percent of the churchgoers had switched from a nondenominational church. One partial explanation for this is new nondenominational congregations tend to draw a large proportion of their constituents from discontented churchgoers while denominationally affiliated congregations tend to attract contented churchgoers and new residents to the community who switch brand loyalty.

Another significant pattern was among the self-identified Pentecostals. Nearly one-third (30 percent) had switched to Pentecostalism, but only one-fifth (19 percent) of the Pentecostals had switched to another religious tradition.

Why Not Both?

In 1960 the husband-wife couple with four children debated, "The time has come to trade in our car. Should we buy a four-door sedan or a station wagon? Most of the mileage will be driving alone to work and back, but when we take the kids or go on vacation, we really need more room." "You're right, let's trade the old clunker in for a new station wagon."

Forty years later the couple with two children resolved that issue by purchasing a minivan for the wife and a sedan or pickup for the husband to drive to work. One consequence was in 2000 more new single-family detached houses were constructed with a two-vehicle attached garage than ever before, and those with a three-car garage outnumbered those new houses built with a one-car garage.

Another consequence is the old standard for that suburban church averaging six hundred at worship on Sunday morning called for one to two hundred off-street parking spaces. The new standard calls for three hundred to 350 spaces. Who expects that husband-wife couple with a seventeen-year-old and a twelve-year-old to come to church in only one motor vehicle? The answer, of course, is adults born before 1920.

The parents of that couple, both of whom were born in the 1930s, discussed where they wanted to live in their retirement years. Should we stay in our familiar surroundings up north in the Frostbelt? Or sell this house and retire to the Sunbelt? The easy answer is to retain the home they have been living in for a couple of decades or longer and enjoy a home in the Sunbelt for three or four months every winter. They continue as loyal members of their home church "up north" and faithfully worship with the same congregation in the Sunbelt every winter.

Their seventeen-year-old granddaughter, who has survived that dangerous year of being sixteen, sees her grandparents modeling the concept of being loyal constituents of two different congregations and reflects, "That's cool! If they can to that, I can, too. I'll go to Sunday school and church every Sunday morning with my parents, but I'm going to drop out of that boring Sunday evening youth fellowship. My two close friends, Pat and Taylor, have been urging me for weeks to come join the Sunday evening youth group in their church." The granddaughter carries out her plan and quickly concludes she has made a wise decision. Her parents reluctantly conclude it is better to see their teenage daughter eagerly looking forward to Sunday evening at that "other church" rather than have to plead with her to attend the youth program in their own church. Several months later the daughter informs her parents she also is going to be a member of a new Wednesday evening high-expectation Bible study group in a third church. "Grandpa and Grandma can go to two different churches every year, why can't I go to three every week?"

Another pattern is the couple who now worships with a megachurch on Saturday evening, but never miss attending the adult Sunday school class in their home church they joined back in 1979.

The Proliferation of Institutions

The United Nations was chartered in 1945 with fifty-one nations. Seven more nations joined in 1946. By June 2002 the UN had 190 member nations. What happened?

The demand for self-determination, self-rule, and freedom from the control of those in distant positions of authority more than tripled the number of independent and autonomous nations on this planet. A total of forty-two became independent during the 1960s compared to only seven during the 1950s and eighteen during the 1940s. Another sixty-five became independent during the 1970–2000 era.

At the end of 2000 the ten most populous nations reported a combined population of 3.8 billion or three-fifths of this planet's 6.3 billion residents. At the other end of the size scale, the least populous ninety-six nations, or slightly more than one-half of all countries, reported a combined population of 235 million, or 3.7 percent of that 6.3 billion total. The largest narrowly defined cluster consisted of the twenty-five autonomous nations with a population in the twenty-to-forty-nine million bracket. Together they include slightly less than one-tenth of the planet's population.

Those three paragraphs may raise interesting questions about who controls the policymaking processes in the United Nations, but what does that have to do with Protestant Christianity in the United States?

In 1900 the overwhelming majority of Christian congregations were affiliated with a religious tradition that traced its origins back to Western Europe. For 1906 the United States Bureau of the Census reported a total of 210,418 religious congregations in America of which 194,497 were labeled "Protestant." Roman Catholics accounted for another 12,472 congregations, Jews 1,152, the Latter-day Saints 1,184, Eastern Orthodox 411, and "all others" 702. Out of that Protestant total of 194,497 congregations, only 1,065 were identified as "Independent" while 2,537 congregations were Adventists, 635 were Church of Christ, Scientist, 10,909 were Christian or Disciples, 435 were Unitarians, Universalists numbered 811, and 3,637 congregations were placed in a category called "other Protestant bodies." Those numbers suggest that four out of five of those Protestant congregations were affiliated with a religious tradition that originated in Western Europe such as Lutheran, Methodist, Evangelical, Episcopal, Presbyterian, Baptist, Congregational, Reformed, Mennonite, Friends, and several dozen other Western European religious traditions. The twentieth century brought a proliferation of religious bodies in America paralleling the proliferation of nations on this planet.

One consequence was the emergence of scores of new "made in America" religious traditions such as the Assemblies of God, the Church of God in Christ, the Vineyard Christian Fellowship, and scores of other new movements, associations, and denominations.

That increase in competition helps to explain why several mainline Protestant denominations with a strong Western European religious heritage peaked in numbers in the years after World War II. Another part of the explanation was the decision by the United States government in 1965 to discourage immigration from Western Europe and to encourage immigration from Latin America and Asia. At least equally influential was the decision by several mainline Protestant denominations to cut back sharply on planting new missions to reach and serve new generations and recent immigrants. (See appendix F.)

Another significant factor was the hope that the arithmetic of denominational mergers called for five plus three to equal nine or ten, and at least eight. The historical record suggests that in American Protestant Christianity the arithmetic of mergers for both denominations and congregations in recent decades calls for five plus three to equal somewhere between three and seven.

The resulting vacuum created by that cutback in new church development by the mainline Protestant denominations was filled by a variety of entrepreneurial individuals, the Southern Baptist Convention, Pentecostals, the Assemblies of God, the Church of God in Christ, new movements, associations of churches, independent congregations, and several of the newer and smaller denominations (they tended to plant twenty to thirty new missions for every thousand existing churches compared to a ratio of 2-to-8 per thousand for the mainline denominations).

Another expression of this proliferation of institutions has been the explosive increase in the number and variety of para-denominational and parachurch organizations, profit-driven corporations, publishing houses, retreat centers, research and development agencies, and self-identified teaching churches since World War II. What once was a shortage of resources for congregational leaders has become an abundance.

That paragraph introduces a crucial policy question. Should denominational leaders watch passively as more and more of their congregations turn to parachurch and paradenominational agencies for resources? If we encourage that, will one consequence be an erosion of loyalty to this denomination? Should we also encourage our congregations to turn to nondenominational affinity networks for learning experiences? Or should we create intradenominational affinity networks to resource our congregations?

What Do We Subsidize?

During the past seven decades the United States government has used financial subsidies to encourage desired behavior among the citizens. Examples include subsidies to encourage farmers to adopt soil conservation practices, income tax benefits to encourage home ownership, loans and grants to encourage people to attend college, grants to encourage mothers to stay home and rear their children, grants to scholars to engage in research projects, grants to religious organizations to expand hospitals, to resettle refugees, and to construct and administer housing for the elderly and the poor, subsidies to employers for job training for the unemployed and subsidies to cities to renew deteriorating neighborhoods. A complete list would be thicker than this book. These are recognized as legitimate efforts by government to redistribute income and wealth as part of a larger strategy to encourage desired behavior and desired outcomes.

Dozens of denominations subsidize pensions for retired ministers, efforts to plant new missions, the compensation for pastors of small congregations, continuing education for the clergy, and construction programs for inner city churches. These are part of a larger goal to use the denominational system for the redistribution of income and wealth to produce desired outcomes.

How does your denomination use its program for the redistribution of income and wealth to produce desired outcomes? Does your system reward numerical growth or a decline in membership? Does it reward good stewardship and penalize poor stewardship? Or does it penalize good stewardship and reward poor stewardship? Do financial subsidies go to ventures with a high probability of success? Or to those with a low probability of success?

The proliferation of congregations founded since 1965 also has produced an interesting debate over priorities in the allocation of scarce denominational resources. The historical record of the past four decades suggests it is far more difficult to revitalize a numerically shrinking congregation that traces its history at the same address back to before 1950 and transform it into a congregation averaging more than one thousand at worship than it is to launch a new mission that averages one thousand or more at worship within a decade or two of that first public worship service. It is far more difficult to renew the old than it is to create the new.

Does your system subsidize perpetuating the old or giving birth to the new?

One consequence is a disproportionately large number of the Protestant congregations averaging one thousand or more at worship that either (a) came into existence after 1960 or (b) have relocated their meeting place since 1960 in order to write a new volume in their history. (For those interested in trivia, as recently as 1965 the most common first name of the megachurches of that era was First: First Baptist, First Presbyterian, First Methodist, or First Reformed. Today, except for Southern Baptists, relatively few megachurches carry a name beginning with the word "First.")

A more significant consequence of that combination of affluence and the proliferation of institutions can be summarized in the question, "What do we subsidize out of our denominational budget?" The traditional response to that question includes (a) any line item that has earned a place in our denominational budget for at least three consecutive years, (b) dying institutions, (c) causes and movements that symbolize our support for egalitarianism, (d) institutions founded by dead white males before World War II and we attempt to retain their allegiance to our religious tradition by sending them money every year, (e) other denominational agencies that have become financially dependent on our annual contributions (this is an effective way to enhance dependency), and (f) organizations and causes that squeak the loudest must be greased, especially if their advocates help prepare the denominational budget.

When those forces come into conflict with the trend described earlier of younger generations preferring to give their charitable dollars directly to an attractive cause rather than to an institution, the result strikes some observers as a paradox. The number of charitable dollars being contributed each year keeps on climbing, but the budgets of institutions are being squeezed. Is that really a paradox, or is it really a predictable consequence of decades of teaching Christians to be responsible stewards?

The highly visible example is that as the size of the federal budget increases, the demands for subsidies to perpetuate the old increases, taxpayers rebel against their tax burden—and give hundreds of millions of dollars to specific causes such as the relief of the victims of 9/11.[6]

Both regional and national denominational agencies are being forced to choose from among competing demands for financial subsidies. Affluence is forcing denominational leaders to respond to two important policy questions. First, what are the criteria that will be used in the allocation of scarce financial resources. Second, do we continue to retain control over the ultimate destination of those charitable dollars or do we create a system that enables the donor to choose that ultimate destination?

They're Bigger than They Used to Be!

With relatively few exceptions, such as computers, nations, telephones, camcorders, armies, radios, and women's skirts, nearly everything else is larger than it was in earlier years. That long list of what is larger ranges from babies to basketball players to backyards.

This raises a crucial policy question for denominational policymakers. Do you believe the future for your denomination is with small and midsized congregations averaging fewer than 350 at worship? Or do you believe the future lies with the larger churches? (For the calendar year 2000 most of the larger American Protestant denominations that ask their congregations to report average worship attendance found that the largest 40 percent of their congregations accounted for somewhere between 72 percent and 85 percent of all worshipers on the typical weekend.)

Are you convinced that direct services to congregations by denominational agencies must be subsidized while congregational leaders are willing to pay full cost for services provided by parachurch organizations and profit-driven corporations?

How do you design your denominational system to be supportive of your desired outcomes?

From Assimilation to Pluralism

Mature readers may recall when "the melting pot" analogy was used to describe how the United States effectively absorbed immigrants from other lands.[7] The big exception, of course, was skin color and turned out to be a high barrier to making that a universal prescription. The combination of affluence and the demand for self-determination has produced an affirmation of ethnic separation that now competes with the goal of racial integration. Multiculturalism has become the politically correct term. Cultural pluralism has become the new mantra to replace assimilation into the melting pot. Many American Protestant congregations have adopted their own version of "We welcome everyone." One version is, "We welcome everyone who worships the same God we worship." Others are more specific, "We welcome everyone who accepts Jesus Christ as lord and savior." A more inclusive slogan is, "We welcome everyone who will welcome everybody." The unwritten sign in front of several church buildings declares, "We welcome everyone who can climb stairs." Another invisible sign suggests, "We welcome everyone who likes our kind of music."

A more useful conceptual framework for both congregations and denominations begins by recognizing that one consequence of affluence is most Americans believe they have the right to expect a "good match" when shopping for a motor vehicle, a sweater, a house or apartment, a television program, a restaurant, a computer, eye glasses, shoes, a future spouse (arranged marriages are rare in America today), a medical prescription, a checking account, a college dormitory, a job, or a church home.

The second step is to distinguish between ideological pluralism and demographic diversity. This introduces a concept articulated many years ago by Alvin Toffler.[8] He explained that in times of change everyone needed what he identified as a "personal stability zone." A stability zone offers continuity with the past, predictability, reassurance, and familiarity.

A simple example is when the congregation that has been worshiping in the same building since 1925 decides to relocate and construct new and larger facilities on a larger site at a better location a few miles distant. One consequence is the people experience the effects of radical change. One way to minimize the impact is for the pastor, who arrived ten years before the relocation, to continue as the pastor for at least several more years. Changing locations and changing pastors in the same year would be double disruption. The continuity of ministerial leadership provides people with a stability zone. For many adults their Sunday school class or mutual support group cushions the shock created by a change in pastors or the relocation of the meeting place.

How does a denomination increase the degree of demographic diversity in its constituency? What should be part of a larger strategy to become a multicultural and multigenerational denomination? Today there are many roads to that goal of creating a multicultural denomination.[9]

The obvious answer is to provide the constituency with a stability zone in the theological and doctrinal position of that denomination. Current American examples include the Church of God in Christ, the Christian and Missionary Alliance, and the Church of Jesus Christ of Latter-day Saints. All three display a substantial degree of demographic diversity and doctrinal uniformity.

On the other hand, the Southern Baptist Convention, The United Methodist Church, the Evangelical Lutheran Church in America, and the Presbyterian Church (U.S.A.) currently stand out as four denominations that are seeking to increase the demographic diversity within the constituency while becoming increasingly ideologically pluralistic. Where do the constituents find their stability zone? One answer is to attempt to ignore the ideological conflicts within their denominational system. Another is for each congregation or regional judicatory to decide, "We'll pay our franchise tax, but go our own way." A third alternative is to table the Great Commission and engage in that intradenominational quarrel over ideology.

A fourth, but much rarer response is for each congregation to repeatedly and clearly articulate its own ideological and theological stance as the stability zone it offers people and concentrate on expanding its demographic diversity. With one major reservation that response enables the denomination to become both ideologically pluralistic and demographically diverse. The reservation is that the parish clergy and lay delegates from congregations should not be asked to attend a denominational meeting more frequently than once every twenty-five years. One price tag on ideological pluralism is the recovery time following attendance at a regional or national denominational meeting is much longer than it was in 1950.

The most popular congregational response is to ignore the divisive nature of both ideological pluralism and demographic diversity. The necessary comfortable, reliable, and reassuring stability zone is the quality and depth of that individual's continuing social network of seven to forty persons. This may be the chancel choir, an adult Sunday school class, a Tuesday evening Bible study and prayer cell, a mutual support group, or a mission task force.

A common example is the small congregation averaging ten to thirty-five at worship with one or two multigenerational families at the hub of that network of interpersonal relationships. Preachers come and go, and their theological stance, age, marital status, ideological concerns, education, credentials, and political affiliation will have little impact. All the members ask is they be reasonably polite, excel in conducting funerals, respect local traditions, carefully avoid forcing the members to choose up sides on a divisive issue,[10] speak the language of the people, and not attempt to change "how we do church here."

While it has received relatively little attention, one of the most significant consequences of the recent affirmation of pluralism can be found in the goals of the ecumenical movement. Literally hundreds of denominational leaders in the twentieth century interpreted the New Testament to include a call for all churches to come together as one institutional expression of God's creation on earth.[11] For most of the twentieth century the goal of Christian unity included a reduction in the number of American Protestant denominations through mergers. As usual the Canadians were ahead of the Americans with the creation of the United Church of Canada in 1925. The 1920–1990 era south of that border was marked by more than three dozen denominational mergers in American Protestantism. By the late 1950s the promotion of denominational mergers had moved above new church development on the agendas of several denominations. (See appendix F.)

The recent affirmation of pluralism plus several hundred funerals have replaced that earlier goal of denominational mergers with a new emphasis on interdenominational cooperation. One consequence was the last rites for the Consultation on Church Union were held in early 2002 and the birth of a new focus on interchurch cooperation was celebrated that same day.

This observer's hunch is that from the perspective of the church historians of 2150, the twentieth century will stand out as an era marked by denominational mergers while the twenty-first century will be described as an era of schisms and the birth of new Christian bodies in America. (Fortunately no one alive in 2150 will be aware of this prediction!)

A More Competitive Marketplace

Affluence has eroded traditional institutional loyalties. One facet of that has been the weakening of residents' loyalties to neighborhood institutions. The neighborhood drugstore, the neighborhood motion picture theater, the neighborhood doctor, the neighborhood grocery store, the neighborhood post office, the neighborhood school, and the neighborhood church are among the institutions affected by that change.

One of the most interesting contemporary examples of the increase in competition has been the creation of "fast-casual" sandwich shops to compete with the traditional "hamburger and fries" fast food restaurants. Within that new genre of fast-casual is a battle over customization. What do customers prefer? Three or four minutes in line while the help builds a customized sandwich to the customer's order? Or no more than ninety seconds in line as Pret a Manger promises a choice among a variety of sandwiches built by trained experts and already packaged in a white cardboard box?[12]

Should the plans for that new church building, which do include space for a coffee bar, be designed for the sale of customized sandwiches or for sandwiches already built and packaged by experts?

The most highly visible factor in creating a more competitive marketplace has been the transformation of personal transportation. In 1900, as in 1800, for most Americans three miles was about the maximum viable journey to work, to school, to a grocery store, to the doctor, to the post office, to the blacksmith shop, to a community hall for social gatherings, to the bank, or to church.

A century later, in 2000, many Americans were comfortable with a seven-to-fifteen mile journey to similar destinations. If the providers of goods, services, and jobs were geographically scattered on a uniform basis, a circle with a ten-mile radius would include eleven times as many vendors, employers, and churches as a circle with a three-mile radius. The geographical distribution is not uniform, but the larger that circle, the greater the competition. A circle with a fifteen-mile radius, for example, includes twenty-two times the area covered by that circle with a three-mile radius. The church shopper who is willing to travel six miles each way to church may have nine times as many choices as those who limit their search to a two-mile radius.

The combination of affluence and the resulting increase in individual discretionary income plus the expansion of the size of that circle raises the probability the individual will be able to find the perfect match, "This is exactly what I was seeking!"

Affluence has increased the size of that circle called a service center. Affluence also has enabled the vendors of goods and services to improve the quality of their product. That has enhanced competition.

Affluence also has enabled those vendors to place a greater emphasis on customer service. That has enhanced competition.

The combination of affluence and larger institutions has enabled vendors (medical clinics, educational institutions, grocery stores, motion picture theaters, discount stores, hospitals, home builders, amusement parks, retirement centers, bookstores, and churches) to increase the range of choices they offer consumers. That has enhanced competition.

One of the consequences of enhanced competition is a new set of winners and losers. Old First Church downtown sent out three hundred members in 1951 to be the nucleus for a new mission on the west side of town. The design called for that new mission to focus on the same segment of the churchgoing population as First Church was serving. Ten years later with a new building on a five-acre site with an abundance of off-street parking, in extensive seven-day-a-week ministry, and a highly skilled program staff, that new mission had surpassed First Church in attendance. A decade or two later the aging leadership at First Church decided to sell their downtown real estate and merge with that daughter congregation.

Television came along to provide viewers with a summary of the day's news. One consequence was in 1950 twelve daily newspapers were sold for every ten homes in the United States, but fifty years later that ratio had dropped to 5.3 daily newspapers sold for every ten American homes.

A parallel consequence is in the typical week an average of at least sixty Protestant congregations disappear from the American ecclesiastical scene through dissolution or by merging into another church. Competition kills off about half of all new missions before they reach their tenth birthday.

A countertrend to large-scale institutions has been made possible by this rising level of affluence. This is the emergence of the niche business that concentrates on responding to the needs of a narrowly and precisely defined slice of the population. Examples include the greeting card store, the coffee bar, the fast-casual sandwich shop, the dentist who specializes in the care of children, restaurants, the small church that serves recent immigrants from Korea, the gift shop, the private building inspector who inspects homes for sale, the church that focuses on ministries with mature adults, the donut shop, the congregation composed largely of homosexual adults, the union-sponsored credit union, the landowner who grows and sells Christmas trees, and the congregation that specializes in ministries with home-schooling families. Affluence has made possible the niche vendor and that has enhanced the level of competition.

This combination of affluence, higher expectations, and competition has had a tremendous impact on where Americans go to church. During the last third of the twentieth century well over 100,000 new Protestant congregations were launched. The majority did not survive to celebrate their tenth birthday, but hundreds of others grew into megachurches.

One consequence was a redistribution of the church-going population. The best way to measure that is to compare a comprehensive census of churchgoers on a typical weekend in one year with a similar census two or three decades later. A few of those data bases are available for a particular city or county, but not for a state or the entire country.

A distant second best approach is to take the reported total membership for each of several denominations, calculate each of those numbers as percentage of the nation's population for that year, and repeat that process for a subsequent year. One major limitation of this methodology is denominations use different definitions of membership. That limits interdenominational comparisons. The membership total for the denomination that practices infant baptism and reports a baptized membership total cannot be compared with the numbers from a denomination that reports confirmed membership totals.

A second limitation surfaces for intradenominational comparisons if that particular denomination changes the definition of membership between the two dates used for comparisons.

For this discussion the "inclusive membership" figures for 1965 and 2000 are used. The 1965 inclusive membership number has been divided by 195 million, the population of the United States in 1965. The inclusive membership number for 2000 was divided by 282 million. For a few religious traditions the membership figures reported in *The Census of Religious Bodies of 1906* conducted by the United States Bureau of the Census are used and divided by 85 million, the population of the United States in 1906.

What do these calculations reveal? In 1906 the reported membership of the Southern Baptist Convention was equal to 2.36 percent of the American population. By 1965 that proportion had more than doubled to 5.7 percent, the same proportion as for 2000. By contrast, the membership of the Church of Jesus Christ of Latter-day Saints in 1906 (216,000) was equal to only one-fourth of one percent of the nation's population. By 1965 that proportion had quadrupled to 1.1 percent, and in 2000 it was up to 1.67 percent.

Back in 1906 the four predecessor denominations of what today is the United Church of Christ reported a combined membership of slightly more than 1.4 million or 1.6 percent of the population. By 1965 that proportion had dropped to 1 percent, and in 2000 it was 0.8 percent.

The comparable proportions for the Episcopal Church in the United States were slightly more than one percent in 1906, 1.7 percent in 1965, and 0.82 percent in 2000.

Denominational mergers do complicate this approach since a significant number of affiliated congregations often decide not to participate in that merger. One example is what today is The United Methodist Church. In 1906 the six predecessor denominations included slightly more than 57,000 congregations with a combined total of nearly 5.3 million members. They represented 6.2 percent of the American population in that year, down from nearly 8 percent in 1860. By 1965 the combined membership of the two predecessor denominations had passed eleven million and was equal to 4.25 percent of the American population. For 2000 the number of congregations had decreased to 35,469, and the membership was 8.4 million or 3 percent of the population.

The members of the four predecessor bodies of what today is the Presbyterian Church (U.S.A.) represented 1.9 percent of the population in 1906. By 1965 that proportion had climbed to slightly more than 2 percent, but in 2000 it was down to 1.25 percent.

The impact of denominational mergers has made it difficult to calculate the historical trend for the Evangelical Lutheran Church in America, but in 1906 the two dozen Lutheran denominations reported 2.1 million communicants scattered among 12,703 parishes. That was equivalent to 2.5 percent of the population. In 1965 the baptized membership of all Lutheran parishes in the United States represented 4.7 percent of the population, and the confirmed membership was equal to 3.1 percent. By 2000 those two proportions were approximately 3 percent and 2.2 percent. In 2000 the baptized membership of the ELCA represented 1.81 percent of the population and the confirmed membership was equal to 1.3 percent. The steamships of one hundred years ago carried more immigrants from Germany and Scandinavia than today's jet airlines bring.

Another complicating factor in calculating historical trends is the changing definition for an "affiliated congregation." This is a significant variable in the United Church of Christ, the Southern Baptist Convention, and other denominations, but it is especially significant with the historical record of the Christian Church (Disciples of Christ). The restructuring of 1968 broke the continuity of the statistical records. In 1906 the Disciples of Christ reported 8,293 congregations with 982,701 members who represented 1.16 percent of the population. The inclusive membership of 1968 was equal to 0.8 percent of the population. In 2000 the inclusive membership of 820,286 was equal to 0.3 percent of the population.

The definition of affiliated congregations also is a factor in looking at the statistical record of the American Baptist Churches in the U.S.A. In 1906 the Northern Baptist Convention reported nearly 1.1 million members in 8,272 congregations. They represented 1.2 percent of the American population. By 1965 that proportion had declined to 0.75 percent, and in 2000 the 1,436,909 members in 5,756 congregations represented 0.51 percent of the American population.

Among the smaller Protestant denominations the Christian and Missionary Alliance doubled the proportion of the American population who are members from 0.59 percent in 1965 to 1.29 in 2000. The Evangelical Free Church in America increased its membership from 6,952 in 127 congregations in 1906 to 125,500 in 1,224 congregations in 1995, and the Evangelical Covenant Church grew from 20,760 members in 281 congregations to 101,000 in 800 congregations in 2000. These two represent the Americanization of a Swedish immigrant church into an evangelical American denomination.

The Unitarians and Universalists reported a combined total of 135,000 members (0.16 percent of the population) in 1,307 congregations in 1906. In 2000 the Unitarian Univeralist Association reported 220,000 members (0.078 percent of the population) in 1,051 congregations.

The Church of the Nazarene increased the number of congregations in the United States from 4,674 with 365,000 members (0.19 percent of the population) in 1968 to 5,070 congregations with 637,000 members (0.23 percent) in 2000.

That census of 1906 reported 74,000 members in 1,079 independent or nondenominational churches. That almost certainly was an undercount due to the methodology. The big increase in the number of nondenominational Protestant congregations, however, did not come until after World War I and especially after 1965. As pointed out earlier, this trend was fed by affluence, the replacement of small neighborhood institutions by large regional centers, consumerism, the demand for self-determination and local control, the erosion of traditional institutional loyalties, and the decision by several of the mainline Protestant denominations after the late 1950s to cut back on new church development.

How many nondenominational Protestant Christian congregations exist in the United States today? No one knows. If one excludes those small lay-led house churches and storefronts, a conservative estimate is twenty thousand independent congregations with at least fifteen million constituents of all ages. That averages out to one in sixteen Protestant churches—and that explains why this is a conservative estimate. A total of fifteen million constituents is equal to only 5 percent of the population. If the reader argues the real numbers are closer to forty thousand nondenominational churches (including those affiliated with a movement or a loose association of churches) with thirty million constituents (many of whom are still carried on the membership rolls of a Protestant denominationally affiliated church or a Roman Catholic parish) that could be a closer reflection of contemporary reality.

A reasonable estimate is somewhere between 8 and 15 percent of all Americans are worshiping with an independent Protestant congregation on the typical weekend in 2003. That is close to the combined worship attendance for all the seventy-five thousand congregations affiliated with the Southern Baptist Convention and The United Methodist Church on that same weekend. Add in those Protestant Christians who are worshiping with a church affiliated with a denomination that traces its origins after that census of religious bodies of 1906 (the Assemblies of God, the Church of God in Christ, the Church of the Nazarene, the International Church of the Foursquare Gospel, et al.), and it is easy to explain the decrease in "market share" of several of the mainline denominations.

The number of Americans worshiping with a Protestant congregation on the typical weekend in 2002 probably was double the equivalent figure of fifty-five years earlier. This combination of more competition and new generations with higher education has produced a radical redistribution of the churchgoing population.[13]

One consequence is the Protestant congregation that earned a grade of B on the quality and range of its ministries in 1955 was able to compete with other churches for potential future constituents. If it offers the identical quality and range of ministries today that it offered in 1955, the generations born after 1950 probably will give it a grade of C or lower. That grade is too low to compete in today's highly competitive ecclesiastical marketplace! On the contemporary ecclesiastical scene, competition is the name of the game.

In 1958, when he described coming age of affluence, John Kenneth Galbraith repeatedly pointed out that affluence increases competition and competition is "the instrument of change."[14] He was right, and that introduces a second paradigm shift.

CHAPTER FIVE

A SECOND PARADIGM SHIFT

O ne of the most significant consequences of affluence is the demand for customization. Rather than purchase a new motor vehicle out of the dealer's stock, the buyer orders one that has the exact combination of optional features to match that customer's preferences. Physicians are relying on computer programs to produce a customized prescription that is compatible with the medications already being taken by that patient as well as to match that patient's unique characteristics and needs. Many adults wear custom-made clothes and shoes. New homes are constructed to match the buyer's preferences. Adult Bible study groups are customized to match a clearly defined constituency. Computers are customized to match the purchaser's needs. Political campaigns are customized to match the gifts and experiences of the candidate and to highlight the deficiencies of the opponent. Instead of a standard core curriculum for that first year or two, first-year college and university students begin their experience in higher education with a customized schedule and choice of courses. Coffee bars offer a customized formula for what once was described simply as a cup of coffee. Fast-food restaurants are selling customized sandwiches. Instead of the farmer spreading the same quantities of mixtures of fertilizers on a field, each section of that field receives a customized application.

On the ecclesiastical scene, however, dependency path theory has encouraged perpetuating educational and training designs that were invented after World War II, long before the competition among congregations for future constituents became a serious issue.

What is the most effective design for equipping pastors, program staff, and lay volunteers to serve in an increasingly diversified and competitive ecclesiastical economy?

One traditional design called for the college graduate to enroll in theological seminary, graduate, and go out to fill the role of the loving shepherd of two small rural congregations. Following a three-to-five year apprenticeship, the next stage called for that person to spend three-to-seven years as the pastor of a congregation averaging eighty-five to 135 at worship. That experience was assumed to be adequate preparation for going next to be the head of staff with a congregation that averaged two to three hundred at worship with the assistance of two or three part-time paid specialists in youth ministries or pastoral care or music or visitation evangelism or Christian education. After fifteen years, more or less, on that career path, it was assumed that the minister was prepared to move on to become the senior minister of a large suburban congregation or Old First Church downtown or perhaps to organize a new congregation. That design called for a pastor periodically to move up on one learning curve, abandon that learning curve to begin near the bottom on a new learning curve, master the skills required for that learning curve, abandon it, and move on to a new learning curve.

Another design called for the regional judicatories and/or national denominational agencies to design and staff one- or two-day "one approach fits everyone" workshops for Christian educators or pastors in a new assignment or choir directors or youth ministers or ministers serving small rural churches or inexperienced church planters.

A parallel change shifted the focus from roles to functions. These one- or two-day events offered by denominational agencies, parachurch organizations, church-related colleges, retreat centers, public universities, theological schools, and councils of churches usually focused on a single theme such as evangelism, stewardship, the Sunday school, ministerial leadership, governance, adult Bible study, fund-raising, or social justice issues. Again one approach was expected to meet everyone's needs, but the participants might come from two dozen different types of congregational environments including the small rural congregation, the downtown church, the large suburban parish, the "arrested development" new mission founded ten years earlier now averaging sixty-five at worship, and the white congregation in a racially changing neighborhood.

By the 1970s that scene began to change. The Board of Homeland Ministries of the United Church of Christ pioneered the concept of an annual four-day event for the senior pastors of very large churches. Several organizations offered narrowly focused training events for leaders of what formerly had been rural farming community congregations, but were now in the process of being transformed into exurban churches. Others created equipping events for teams of congregational leaders who would come together for three days to prepare a customized ministry plan for their congregation. Theological schools that had encouraged a one-year supervised intern year for students now began to require it. Team-building events were being designed for the program staff of large congregations and for church planting teams.

By 1980 the American ecclesiastical scene included a growing variety of training events that were offered by denominational agencies, parachurch organizations, retreat centers, seminaries, and publishing houses and were designed for a relatively narrowly and precisely defined constituency. These, however, tended to be (a) producer-designed and (b) staffed largely by "experts" who were not engaged in the daily practice of parish ministry.

The Teaching Church Has Arrived

By 1990 the new kid on the block had arrived. This was the self-identified teaching church. A small, but growing number of large congregations that had earned a reputation as "a model for the American Protestant church in the twenty-first century" began to design and offer two-to-six-day events. The basic theme of these teaching churches can be summarized in one brief paragraph.

"Come and learn from us. This is what we have invented. It has worked for us and you may want to adapt what we have learned to your situation back home. This event will be staffed completely by our own people, both lay volunteer and paid staff. We are prepared to share with you what we have learned and the mistakes we made that have had to be corrected. We will be glad to answer all your questions, and we expect to learn from you as you push us to explain the why, the what, and the how of our ministry."

Those also are producer-designed events, but the designers and staff are practitioners who are engaged in implementing the same model of ministry. They come from a common background, not from different parish experiences. They bring a degree of internal consistency in values, goals, dreams, plans, and experience that cannot be duplicated by the event staffed by seven people who bring seven different perspectives on how to do ministry in the twenty-first century. The pedagogical design emphasizes peer learning rather than the traditional teacher-student model. The design includes volunteers learning from volunteers carrying similar responsibilities.

Why would any congregation send three to a dozen congregational leaders, usually at considerable expense, to spend three days with the staff of a teaching church?

A common explanation is found in these words. "We have been looking for a contemporary working model of what we believe God is calling our congregation to be in the twenty-first century. Five or ten years ago this teaching church resembled what our congregation is today. Today it resembles what we believe we should be in the future. We want to travel down a road similar to the road they have taken. By studying what they have learned, we believe we can not only move at a faster pace, but also avoid some of the detours and pitfalls they encountered. Our team wants to learn from their team."

Students of environmental psychology will add another advantage possessed by the teaching church. Instead of individual learners meeting in a hotel ballroom with strangers who bring a huge variety of agendas as they gather to listen to a passing parade of experts, the teaching church gathers teams of eager learners in the physical environment that houses the ministries of a worshiping community. The staff are on their home turf. The learners come as teams, not as individuals. The team members learn from one another's questions, reflections, and observations. The physical setting enables them to experience several components of the ministries of the teaching church. Ideally all of the visiting teams come from similar type congregations. These visiting teams, while far from identical in the nature of the churches they represent, do expect to travel down a road into the future that does resemble the road other teams are designing. In addition to learning from the experiences of the teaching churches, these visiting teams can learn from one another.

Finally, this design stands in sharp contrast to the format that calls for a congregation to invite the superstar pastor of a superchurch to "Come and share with us how your congregation became a superchurch." After a combination two-hour lecture and question-and-answer period, the members shake the hand of that superstar and depart. As they go home, one says to another, "That was interesting, but we could never do that here. Those people must be giants and most of the people in our congregation are pygmies."

A common response is, "Maybe that's true, but if we had a superstar leader, we might be able to do more than we're now doing."

As the visiting team heads home from three or four days with the volunteer and paid staff of that teaching church, one of the team members comments, "You know, they have a couple of people there I wish we could rent for a few months to help us, but when you look at their whole team, most of them are shorter, fatter, and uglier than our people. In spite of that, they have a great ministry. I'm convinced our people, who are taller, thinner, more gifted, and better looking, probably can do a better job in the years ahead than they've done."

The big paradigm shift advocated in this book is to encourage congregations to create and benefit from affinity networks or judicatories that bring together congregations that are similar in community context, culture, role, type, size, hopes, dreams, and priorities. That shift would widen the door that only recently was unlocked. That door leads into a worldview that can be nurtured by this teaching church model.

This second paradigm shift calls for adding to that marketplace of educational, learning, and equipping events for congregational leaders this model of peer learning called the teaching church.

As your congregation begins to prepare a customized ministry plan designed to take your church down a particular road into the twenty-first century, where can they turn for help in designing and implementing that customized ministry plan? One alternative is a workshop on how to design a ministry plan. A second is to call in a consultant who specializes in helping congregations prepare ministry plans. A third, and perhaps the most productive, would be to send a team from your congregation to spend three or four days learning from practitioners in a teaching church that already has traveled down a similar road into the future.

Finally, when the time comes for your congregation to search for a successor to your pastor who is about to depart, where do you look? Do you search first among the pastors in your geographically defined regional judicatory, most of whom are now serving a congregation unlike your church? Or do you conduct a national search across your denomination? Or are you free to go outside your denominational family in your search for the ideal candidate?

The affinity network or judicatory opens the door to making the initial search for a successor from among pastors currently serving congregations that resemble your church in terms of culture, type, goals, role, and priorities.

Which will produce the steeper and longer learning curve for that successor?

Is the organizational structure of your denomination designed to encourage or discourage the emergence of intradenominational self-identified teaching churches? Is it designed to encourage or discourage peer learning? Is it designed to produce a long and steep learning curve for a newly arrived pastor? Or to maximize the benefits from that ancient bit of wisdom that declares, "It's always easier the second time."

CHAPTER SIX

WHAT ARE THE DESIRED OUTCOMES?

T he Ford Motor Company is organized to make money for the shareholders and officers. To fulfill that goal, it assembles and sells motor vehicles and loans money to borrowers.

That big supermarket chain is organized to make money for the shareholders and officials. To do that, it operates a few thousand stores that sell groceries and allied products.

Kimberly-Clark is organized to make money for its shareholders and officials. To do that, it manufactures paper, diapers, and other products. To be able to make money in a highly competitive marketplace, it also has to be innovative and open to change. One consequence is today's baby diapers are only one-third the size they were two decades ago, but they are far more absorbent than earlier versions.[1]

Public schools are organized to prepare students for the next stage of their lives by providing relevant learning opportunities. To do that, they spend most of their money on the employment of adults and maintaining real estate.

Cities are organized for the protection of people and property and other public services. To fulfill that purpose, they are authorized to enact and enforce laws, ordinances, and regulations. To pay for those services, they are authorized to levy and collect a variety of taxes and fees for services.

All five are also in the customer service business. All five usually prosper if their constituents are happy with the goods and services they receive. The first three, however, have two big advantages over public schools and cities. Those first three have a relatively objective, easy-to-define, quantifiable, and widely agreed upon criterion for internal self-evaluation. How are we doing? The number-one criterion is not, "Are the customers happy?" The number-one criterion for self-evaluation is called the bottom line. Is this organization making money or losing money? This is usually measured and reported on a quarterly and annual basis.

The second big advantage enjoyed by Ford, that national supermarket chain, and Kimberly-Clark is that everyone in a policymaking position agrees on that definition of the primary purpose and of the yardstick to be used for internal self-evaluation. The customers may prefer to focus on the quality of the service. The employees may prefer to evaluate their employer by working conditions and compensation. Mothers are more interested in diaper rash and convenience than corporate profits, but they are not the policymakers. Scores of profit-driven corporations have left behind a huge cadre of satisfied customers and contented employees when the absence of profits forced them to close their doors.

Those introductory paragraphs suggest three answers to the question: What is the future of your denomination?[2] One answer is the capability to pay its bills. In late 2001 the Anglican Diocese of Cariboo in western Canada closed when it was unable to pay the judgments entered against it. The Anglican Church of

Canada was the defendant in eight hundred lawsuits, and by late 2001 was spending $100,000 a month on legal fees. Several dioceses in the Roman Catholic Church in America have been confronted with huge legal bills and judgments for the wrong doing of parish priests. The legal doctrine of ascending liability may be the newest major threat to traditional denominational systems.

A second answer to that question about the future of your denomination is the central theme of this book. How is it organized? Is the central organizing principle compatible with the American Protestant ecclesiastical scene of 1720? Or 1780? Or 1830? Or 1880? Or 1910? Or 1955? Or 2005?

A third answer to that question is when some of the outcomes of the system become unacceptable. A current example of this issue of mixed outcomes surfaced in the United States during the last third of the twentieth century. The old system of criminal justice was replaced with a new system. The new system is based on a more punitive policy toward criminals, especially those convicted of the possession or sale of addictive drugs. Mandatory-minimum sentences, the "Three strikes and you're out" legislation, and tougher parole policies were among the components of the new system.

One outcome was a quadrupling in the number of persons incarcerated. A second is an even more rapid increase in the number of prisoners past age sixty-five. A third is the drop in the rate of violent crimes as potential second and third offenders are confined to prison.

Systems produce outcomes. A change in the system produces a new set of outcomes.

The Three Temptations

The most common temptation when conditions call for a response to the current state of affairs in a denominational system is to begin on page six of what should be a six-page agenda. That sixth page focuses on means-to-an-end concerns. What are the resources that will be required to implement our strategy? This means identifying the inputs needed to produce those desired outcomes.

When that becomes the initial response to "our problems," it often produces pleas such as these, "We need more money." "We need more staff." "We need greater support from the laity." "We need better in-service training for our pastors." "We need new leadership." "We need more cooperation from our congregations."

A more productive beginning point would be, "We need to agree on why our current ecclesiastical system is not producing the outcomes we desire."

That wish leads us back to page one of this six-page agenda. What are the criteria for defining who the "we" should be in that sentence?

That introduces the second temptation. This is to be sure that every point of view, value system, caucus, interest group, vested interest, theological stance, agency, ethnic group, ideological position, and age cohort will be represented on that ad hoc commission created to study the problem and come up with a recommended action plan.

The use of that criterion for selecting members of that ad hoc group usually leads to (a) pressures to protect bureaucratic turf, (b) trading favors to produce the lowest common denominator compromises, (c) support for perpetuating obsolete or counterproductive denominational traditions, (d) the addition of diversionary items to the agenda, (e) conflict over the priorities in the allocation of scarce resources, (f) reinforcement of the distrust of the initiative, creativity, and wisdom of congregational leaders, and (g) a hope to arrive at a one-size-fits-all solution.

If there is general agreement that the primary reason for the existence of denominational systems is to regulate the belief systems, behavior, and practices of congregations and the clergy, the number-one criterion for selecting members of that ad hoc task force should be an affirmative response to three questions. First, "Do you agree that regulation is the number-one purpose of our denomination?" Second, "Do you agree our present regulatory system needs to be improved and strengthened?" Third, "Do you believe God has called you to be a regulator and also has provided you with the gifts required to be an effective regulator?"

If, however, there is general agreement that the primary purpose of denominational systems is to help congregations fulfill the Great Commission, and that is a central thesis of this book, six of the criteria for selecting members of that task force could resemble these questions.

1. Do you believe the number-one purpose of this denominational system is to help congregations fulfill the Great Commission?

2. Are you open to learning more about the outcomes of our current system?

3. Do you believe an annual performance audit of goals and actual outcomes will be useful in evaluating how effective our denomination has been and is in fulfilling the Great Commission?

4. Are you driven by a passion for evangelism?

5. Do you agree that the American context for ministry in the twenty-first century will be substantially different from the context of the twentieth century and thus may require changes in our system? (See chapter 4 on "What Are the Consequences of Affluence?")

6. Are you open to changing the present system?

The criteria used to select the members of an ad hoc task force or study group or futures committee always have a huge influence on the recommendations generated by that group.

The third temptation is to arrive at recommendations that will make everyone happy. That temptation usually produces one or more of these undesirable outcomes, (a) a dissenting minority report, (b) watered-down compromises that undermine the effectiveness of the recommended action plan, (c) action plans that require far more resources than can be mobilized, and (d) recommendations that "one size will fit all," these often begin with the words, "Every congregation shall . . ." or "It is strongly recommended that every pastor shall . . .", (e) a design that assumes a structure designed to perpetuate the past is compatible with creating a new future (see chapter 8), (f) the dream that every problem has an "everybody wins without any pain" solution, and (g) arguments for opponents to defeat the proposed action plan when it is scheduled for a vote of approval.

With rare exceptions transformational action plans produce winners and losers!

Step Four Is Step Four!

Earlier it was suggested that any effort to restructure a denominational system around the central organizing principle of fulfilling the Great Commission should be seen as a six-step process.

The first step is to agree on the criteria for selecting members of that ad hoc task force. The second step explains why the third chapter in this book deserves early attention. To the optimum degree possible, the members of that task force should share a common perspective on the issues discussed in this chapter. The greater the divergence in their belief systems, the more difficult it will be for them to agree on an internally consistent and coherent action plan.

The third step in that process is illustrated by the contents of the second, third, fourth, and fifth chapters in this book. In simple terms this task force is charged with designing a strategy to move this denominational system from "Here" to "There." In a profit-driven business, "Here" may be a system that is losing money and "There" is a system that promises regular profits. The third step in this process calls for an accurate analysis of why that system is producing financial losses. The fourth step is to identify the sources of those desired profits.

For denominational policymakers that third step calls for an accurate description of the present system including the outcomes it is producing. The fourth step calls for reaching agreement on the desired outcomes. That is the theme of this chapter.

The fifth step is to create a denominational system designed to produce those desired outcomes. (See chapter 7.) A big component of this fifth step is to identify trade-offs. One desirable outcome is incompatible with another more desirable outcome. This book has been written on the assumption that the creation of affinity judicatories can be an influential component of that new system, but that involves trade-offs. (See chapter 12.)

Finally, the sixth step focuses on the means-to-an-end issues including schedules, identifying the inputs into the system that must be mobilized (votes, money, people) and agreement on the sequence of steps in the implementation process.

At this point the impatient reader cries, "But when do we get to the discussion of desirable outcomes?" The answer is only after emphasizing that should be the fourth, not the first, step in this process! What do we mean by desired outcomes?

A Dozen Examples

1. The first of these desired outcomes recognizes the cultural and institutional differences between congregations and denominational agencies. Every congregation has its own distinctive central organizing principle. For example, one congregation may be organized to serve persons who were born in Korea and immigrated to the United States as adults. Two blocks away in another building is the meeting place for a congregation composed largely of Chinese-Americans who were born in the United States to parents who came to the United States as young children. Two blocks away a third building houses another congregation composed largely of mature adults who are third- and fourth-generation Americans of Western European ancestry. All three congregations are affiliated with the same denomination, but they differ greatly in culture and in their central organizing principle.

By contrast, it is reasonable to assume that most of the national agencies and all of the midlevel judicatories of one denomination could share the same central organizing principle—to help congregations fulfill the Great Commission.

It must be acknowledged that brief paragraph does not enjoy

universal support! One dissenting view contends that most of the large denominations operate with several central organizing principles. They are organized to serve as regulatory bodies, to provide a prophetic voice on behalf of their member churches, to operate a pension system for the clergy, to resource congregations, to enlist and support missionaries on other continents, to serve as the basic building block for ecumenism, to promote social justice, to help finance a variety of charitable causes, to lobby governmental agencies, and other purposes. That sentence often is condensed into the term "mission creep."

One of the most powerful barriers to the renewal of these large mainline Protestant denominations is an absence of agreement on the top two or three reasons for the existence of that denomination in the twenty-first century!

The theme of another dissenting view is summarized in the words of the novelist Michael Dibden. "There can be no true friends without true enemies. Unless we hate what we are not, we cannot love what we are." Those two sentences help us understand the motivations of terrorists, the Israeli-Palestinian conflict, major league football, and the emergence of various caucuses and interest groups within several American Protestant denominations.

A third dissent is offered by those who operate on the assumption that congregations exist to resource denominational systems, not the other way around. They count the number of dollars congregations send to denominational headquarters as the primary yardstick for evaluating the performance of affiliated churches.

From this observer's perspective, however, the future of each of today's mainline Protestant denominations will be determined largely by how effective it is in helping congregations fulfill the Great Commission. One reason for making such a bold statement is by the year 2083 most of the current membership will have disappeared.

2. Another highly desirable outcome is to encourage congregational leaders to benefit from the lessons learned by leaders in similar congregations. Instead of joining weakness with weakness in the hope that will produce strength, concentrate on learning

from success. Affinity judicatories can be a way to open that door to learning from one another's successes.

3. Which congregations are most effective in fulfilling the Great Commission? High on the list of variables is an ideal match between the culture, needs, and goals of the congregation that has decided to make that the top priority and the gifts, skills, personality, passion, leadership style, priorities, theological stance, experience, and energy of the current pastor.

Therefore the organizational structure of the denomination should be designed to increase the probability of producing good matches when a congregation welcomes a new pastor.

4. Which is the higher priority in the allocation of scarce resources? (a) To revitalize and renew numerically shrinking and aging congregations? (b) To challenge that five-to-ten-year-old new mission that has plateaued in size with an average worship attendance less than one hundred to transform itself into at least a midsized congregation? (c) To bring together a staff team of three-to-five persons to implement a carefully designed ministry plan that calls for planting a new mission to reach and serve recent immigrants or unchurched American-born residents born after 1960 with the expectation this will be a large church from week one? (d) To encourage numerically growing congregations currently averaging more than eight hundred at worship to expand their outreach and to enlarge their ministry?

The first of these four scenarios is the most difficult to implement. This usually requires a pastor who brings a contagious passion for evangelism, is an exceptionally skilled agent of planned change initiated from within an organization, is a highly productive worker, is comfortable when as many as one-third of the members depart because too many changes are being adopted too rapidly, and is a gifted communicator of the gospel of Jesus Christ. Currently the demand for these ministers exceeds the supply by at least a 20-to-1 ratio.

The demand for ministers who are able to accomplish that second scenario exceeds the supply by at least a 10-to-1 ratio.

While it is not easy to bring together the team required for that third scenario, the success rate for that model exceeds 70 percent.

If that very large congregation enjoys an excellent match between the senior minister (or team leader) and the needs of that congregation, and if there is a real possibility of continuing that match for at least another decade or two, that fourth scenario can be the most productive of the four in fulfilling the Great Commission.

As you define the desirable outcomes for your denominational system, which of these scenarios is at or near the top of that list?

5. What is your preferred approach to gathering twenty thousand people together for the corporate worship of God? Do you prefer a mix of two hundred congregations with one hundred averaging forty at worship, thirty-four averaging one hundred in attendance, fifty averaging 150 at worship, ten averaging two hundred at worship, four averaging 425 each at worship, and two averaging seven hundred each?

Or do you prefer a mix of thirty congregations with ten averaging 350 at worship, twelve averaging five hundred, five averaging one thousand, and three multisite congregations, each averaging nearly two thousand at worship?

We have decades of experience on how to produce a regional judicatory resembling that first one with two hundred congregations and a combined average worship attendance of twenty thousand. During the past two decades we have learned how to create that second mix of thirty congregations.

Which of these two scenarios is the higher one on your list of desired outcomes?

6. A favorite contemporary game among several denominational families is to load the agenda of the meetings of both the national assembly and the regional judicatories with controversial and divisive issues that are decided by fifty-five to forty-five or sixty-to-forty or seventy-to-thirty votes. The larger the number of "losers" produced by these votes, the more difficult it is to rally support for making the Great Commission the number-one priority.

Therefore a desirable outcome could be to create a denominational system that minimizes internal quarreling. A greater reliance on affinity, rather than geographically defined midlevel judicatories is one way to produce that outcome.

7. One of the consequences of affluence is the rising demand for self-determination. That generalization applies to teenagers, retirees, the delivery of health care services, ethnic minority groups, professional athletes, drug users, women, college and university students, the market for mass transit, the American labor force, political parties, and churches.

In 1900, when ten miles was a long trip, it was logical to create midlevel judicatories on the basis of the geographical proximity of the churches. Today, when the differences among congregations are far greater than ever before in American history and transportation is relatively fast and low cost, it is both possible and useful to allow each congregation to choose its own midlevel judicatory. Those who prefer a geographically defined association, conference, diocese, district, presbytery, region, or synod should have that option. Those who prefer a relatively homogeneous affinity midlevel judicatory should have that option.

If a desired outcome is to transform what is still a predominantly Anglo denomination into a multicultural body, that right of self-determination becomes a crucial variable.

8. The most challenging outcome on this list is to encourage theological pluralism. The numerically growing religious bodies in America are noted for certainty, rather than ambiguity in their belief systems. That is NOT a new pattern! If the desired outcomes include both (a) a reduction in internal quarreling and (b) an affirmation of theological pluralism, two of the key variables are an affirmation of the right of self-determination at the congregational level and a greater reliance on affinity-based midlevel judicatories.

9. The trade-off few want to discuss is between differentiation and Christian unity. Should the denominational system be designed to emphasize "what we have in common with other Christian bodies"? Or should it be designed to emphasize "How we differ from other Christian bodies in America"? The religious bodies in America that are most effective in attracting younger

generations tend to affirm differentiation. They project very high expectations of anyone seeking to become a member. They stress certainty, not ambiguity in their belief system. They rarely rely on denominational loyalty as a source of future constituents. They place a high value on the impact of transformational experiences in an individual personal faith pilgrimage.

At this fork-in-the-road, which is the more desirable outcome? To make it easier to go down the road of Christian unity or to encourage differentiation in both denominational and congregational identities?

10. None of today's mainline and predominantly white American Protestant denominations enjoys a large and influential presence in (a) the nation's large central cities and older suburban communities as well as in (b) suburban America, and (c) nonmetropolitan counties.

Which of those should be the top priority in the desired outcomes for your denomination? The answer, "All three," represents either an absence of critical thinking or access to unlimited resources.

11. To return to the last several pages of chapter 2, what is your desired outcome? To increase both the number of constituents and the market share for your denomination? Or to increase the numbers while accepting a decrease in market share? Or simply to reverse the numerical decline of recent years?

12. Finally, one sentence in this book cannot be challenged. The organizational structure of your denomination that earns widespread approval in 2006 will be less acceptable in 2036. Thus one desired outcome could be a degree of flexibility in that design that will make it relatively easy to adapt it to a new set of circumstances in 2016 or 2026 without a prolonged internal struggle.

This is not intended to be either an ideal or an exhaustive list of desirable outcomes. It is offered here for two reasons. One is to illustrate the concept of outcomes. The second is to demonstrate why the desired outcomes should be articulated before designing a new structure and long before identifying the resources on the input side of the ledger that will be required to implement that new ministry plan.

The organizational structure of your denomination should be designed to produce the desired outcomes. The neutral or value-free organizational structure does not exist. That explains why another chapter must be devoted to the impact of polity.

CHAPTER SEVEN

WHAT ABOUT THE POLITY?

For nearly two hundred years the textbook definition of the polity of the institutional expression of the Christian faith in America has been summarized in three words: episcopal, congregational, and presbyterian. (A fourth category, the state-established church, disappeared from the American ecclesiastical scene with the adoption of the eleventh amendment to the state constitution of the Commonwealth of Massachusetts that took effect on January 1, 1834.)

In many of the denominational discussions on Christian unity in the twentieth century, polity emerged as a highly divisive issue. That, however, has been a clergy-dominated debate on the American ecclesiastical landscape. Two blocks away on that same ecclesiastical landscape, the laity have been voting in increasing numbers, with their feet in opposition to the episcopal system.

The exodus of younger generations born into the Roman Catholic Church, The United Methodist Church, and other traditions with an episcopal polity is one expression of the demand for self-determination described in chapter 4. (CAUTION: Disapproval by the laity does not automatically carry the message, "That is wrong!" During the twentieth century in literally thousands of American Protestant congregations, the laity also have disapproved of pastors driving a motor vehicle on the Sabbath, the installation of electricity, indoor plumbing, telephones, video projectors in church buildings, the divorce of clergymen, the relocation of the meeting place, the ordination of women, and the "new music.")

Most of those who voted with their feet to leave a religious tradition with an episcopal polity also voted with their feet to go to a church with a congregational system of governance. Smaller, but significant numbers of religious migrants have left a congregation with a presbyterian polity to join a church with a congregational polity. A smaller proportion of those switchers have joined congregations affiliated with an episcopal or presbyterian system. In other words, for whatever it may mean, in the ecclesiastical voting booths, younger American churchgoers are casting a majority of their votes for congregational polity. The most obvious measurable evidence of this trend has been the emergence of thousands of new and numerically growing nondenominational and independent Protestant churches with a congregational system of governance.

The most highly visible countertrend is found in the Southern Baptist Convention, which has a long history of affirming complete congregational autonomy. In recent years, however, a number of Southern Baptist leaders have identified the limitations of that system and apparently have concluded the time has arrived to adopt a Baptist version of the presbyterian polity. This calls for the Southern Baptist Convention and/or the state conventions to accept the responsibility to regulate the belief systems and practices of both the clergy and congregations. Several Southern Baptist pastors and at least a few dozen lay leaders in congregations continue to insist they are both trustworthy and competent

and therefore should be allowed to make decisions for their congregation on both belief systems and practices. The majority,
however, appear to agree the time has come for the Southern
Baptist Convention to move from a congregational to a presbyterian system of polity.

The larger trend in American Christianity, including in the
Roman Catholic Church, however, appears to be a drift toward
increased local control and a weakening of the episcopal system.
One of the most powerful forces behind this trend is the product
of a natural, normal, and predictable bureaucratic syndrome. The
longer a particular bureaucratic system has been in existence
and/or the larger that system and/or the greater the degree of hetereogeneity among the components of that system, the greater
the pressure to adopt rules that will strengthen the regulatory
authority of officials in control of that system. Instead of func-
tioning in a servant-leadership role designed to undergird and
strengthen the ministry of the affiliated congregations, the temptation is to redefine that as a master-leader role and regulate the
practices and behavior of both the clergy and congregations.

One example of that syndrome made the national news in
early 2002 when Cardinal Francis George of the archdiocese of
Chicago decided the time had come to reassign Father Michael
Pfleger, the pastor of St. Sabina Parish, a predominantly African
American but multicultural church on Chicago's south side.
Three decades earlier that archdiocese had adopted a rule limit-
ing clergy assignments to two consecutive six-year terms. In
November 2001 Father Pfleger had completed three six-year
terms. Therefore he must be reassigned. Nearly everyone agreed
this white priest has been an ideal match for this parish.

Which should guide the placement process? The needs of the
parish? Or the rules of the archdiocese, which have been waived
on other occasions? Which is the higher priority? To reinforce
the authority of the episcopal leadership? Or to undergird, reinforce, and continue an outstanding ministry? That debate has
encouraged many of the laity to abandon the episcopal system.

This apparent erosion of lay support for an episcopal system of
church government is not confined to the Roman Catholic

Church! This demand for greater local control also can be seen all across American Protestantism. It has evoked a huge variety of responses from among the leaders in American Christianity. Most of these responses can be summarized in seven sentences.

1. That is not true! (Denial.)
2. This trend clearly is contrary to God's will!
3. If it is true, how can we reverse it!
4. In the long run, is this good or bad?
5. While it may be an accurate summary of a basic trend, it is of little importance because the Second Coming of Christ is only a few months away.
6. I'll be dead within a few years, so why should I be concerned?
7. What have been the forces behind this trend?

This observer is convinced that last response is the one that will shed the most light on the central themes of this book.

It appears the episcopal system of governance in American Christianity has been undermined by several forces including (1) egalitarianism,[1] (2) the growing popularity of flat organizational systems to replace the old hierarchical systems, (3) education of the laity, (4) increasing complexity of congregational life that has demanded customized responses to difficult problems instead of the application of standard one-size-fits-all rules, (5) the expanding range of demands and expectations placed on the office of bishop that means it is now unreasonable to expect one person will possess the gifts, skills, personality, passion, time, energy, vision, experience, perspective, and wisdom to be able to earn a grade of "satisfactory" in the performance of those duties, (6) the increasing degree of differences among the congregations affiliated with the regional judicatory served by that bishop, (7) the contemporary quest to increase the degree of diversity and pluralism within one religious tradition, (8) the combination of (a) the higher level of competence required for a minister to be an effective pastor in 2003 compared to what was required in 1953 (the level of performance that earned a grade of B in 1953 now receives a grade of D) and (b) the national shortage of Christian ministers equipped to meet that higher standard, (9) the easy access of the laity to sermons through radio and television from preachers of other Christian traditions, (10) the increasing worldwide demand for the right of self-determination and control of one's own future, (11) the growing adversarial relationships between many of the very large congregations and their denominational headquarters, (12) affluence and consumerism have eroded the old loyalty to producer-driven systems, (13) the old culture assumed authority was automatically granted to the person holding an office such as mayor, tribal chief, college president, pastor, governor, corporate chief executive officer, foreman, bishop, and teacher while the contemporary American culture has declared authority must be earned and re-earned, (14) the impact of the decisions by the United States Supreme Court in Baker v. Carr (1962) and Reynolds v. Sim (1964) that affirmed a civil system of representative government, (15) the emergence of investigative reporting that exposes the shortcomings of persons in offices of great authority, (16) the demands of ecumenism, (17) the long-term gradual democratization of American Christianity,[2] (18) the growing assumption among American churchgoers that denominations should see themselves as voluntary associations rather than as covenant communities and the episcopal system is compatible with a covenant community, but not with a voluntary association of congregations, (19) the legal liability of headquarters in an episcopal system of church government and the potential for substantial financial awards to plaintiffs and their legal counsel, and (20) perhaps most influential in the Western world since 1500, the combination of the decision to translate Holy Scripture into the language of the people and the invention of movable type that have made the Bible available to the common people.

One response to that long list is the role of bishops in a democratic society is now a more time-consuming, stress-producing, demanding, and difficult assignment than ever before in the history of Christianity.

A second American response is the recent great improvements in transportation and communication have more than offset those other forces. They have transformed this into a relatively easy assignment. (Does anyone really believe that?)

The pragmatic response in America after World War II was this assignment has outgrown the time, energy, talents, gifts, and competence of any one person. It has evolved into a 180-hour work week.

A fourth response has been the recent increase in the number of pastors of nondenominational and independent congregations who carry the title "bishop" or "archbishop."[3]

A Key Fork in the Road

That pragmatic response opened two doors to the future. One called for narrowing the definition of the bishop's responsibilities. The other called for adding staff to help carry that expanding workload. That second door replaced the one-room office in the bishop's residence with a suite of offices and a staff. The staff included a secretary to help with correspondence, an administrative assistant to handle a variety of other details, and an assistant bishop to carry part of that growing workload.

The definition of the problem was to maintain the office of bishop as the viable hub of the polity. This was a natural, normal, and predictable institutional response to the problem. Provide additional resources to the input side of the system to continue its viability.

A different definition of the problem begins with Matthew 28:19. What is the number-one purpose of a denominational system? To maintain "our historic polity" for the benefit of generations yet to be born or to fulfill the Great Commission?

If scarce financial resources are to be allocated to hiring more staff, what is the number-one qualification of those staff members? Is it to carry part of the bishop's workload? Or to help congregations fulfill the Great Commission? If the bishop has three assistants, is it fair to hold that bishop accountable for errors in judgment or decision making of each of those assistants? Should that new staff member be seen as an extension of the bishop's office? Or should it be someone with the gifts, skills, experience, wisdom, personality, passion, energy, and creativity to work with congregational leaders in designing and implementing a customized ministry to enable that congregation to fulfill the Great Commission?

Those are radically different assignments! They call for two different sets of gifts. They also generate two radically different sets of expectations. The bishop's assistant probably will have an office in the same building that houses the episcopal office. The congregational consultant may live and work out of an office in a different county or even in another state.

In specific terms this raises a question for the Evangelical Lutheran Church of America. Should each professional synod staff member be seen as a generalist? Or as a specialist in one phase of helping congregations fulfill the Great Commission? Or should one serve as a pastor to pastors? Should another specialize in ministerial placement? Should one specialize in raising money to fund denominational causes and agencies? Should every staff member be expected to be competent in working with all sizes and types of parishes? Or should each be a specialist?

A similar set of questions are raised when the subject is the role of the United Methodist district superintendent. Should that person's office be in the same building that houses the bishop's office? Or in a church building in that superintendent's district? What is the number-one gift and skill required of a United Methodist district superintendent? To be able to persuade all congregations to pay their apportionments in full? To serve as a pastor to pastors? To excel in the ministerial placement process? (That raises a conflict of role with serving as pastor to pastors.) To excel in planting new missions? To excel in designing the appropriate staff configuration for very large churches? To assist pastors and congregational leaders in solving difficult problems? To be a counselor with pastors serving a two- or three-church circuit? To promote the denominational program? To excel in conflict resolution? To carry out the current bishop's agenda and priorities? To excel in the design of new church buildings? To challenge congregational leaders with a vision of a new tomorrow? To broker resources from various vendors?

A parallel set of questions can be asked when the issue of staffing the presbytery tops the agenda. Is the primary role of the executive presbyter to make sure the responsibilities of that presbytery are fulfilled decently and in order? Or to regulate congregational beliefs, practices, and strategies? What is the number-one criterion for evaluating congregations? By attendance of elders at presbytery meetings? By how effectively that congregation is fulfilling the Great Commission? By the willingness and effectiveness of volunteers serving on presbytery committees? By the number of dollars that congregation sends to presbytery? By the number and quality of the candidates for full-time Christian vocations enlisted by that congregation? By how well it treats its pastor? By the number of new missions that congregation has planted in the past decade? By the number of lay volunteers for short-term missionary assignments outside North America each year? By the annual increase or decrease in average worship attendance?

The End of an Era?

Does this mean the episcopal system of church government no longer has a future in American Christianity?

Absolutely not!

The episcopal system was challenged in Western Europe in the sixteenth century. Five hundred years later it is still alive. More recently it has been challenged in South America, Africa, and North America, but it is still alive on those continents.

The episcopal system of government also can provide material for those who derive great personal satisfactions from intradenominational quarrels. This can be a more attractive agenda item than discussing a strategy to help congregations fulfill the Great Commission. One contemporary example is among those who trace their denominational traditions back at least thirteen centuries. How should an American Christian interpret the canons of the Council of Nicaea of 325? Only a few disagree with the canon that prohibits self-castration by the clergy. In the Evangelical Lutheran Church in America the clergy, however, disagree over whether adoption of the Nicene Creed also requires following other canons that came out of the Council of Nicea. Does this mean newly elected bishops must be ordained rather than simply installed? Does Canon IV bind the ELCA?

Most United Methodists agree that the top two qualities for a candidate for the episcopacy should be that minister is (a) a deeply devoted follower of Jesus Christ and (b) a person of good moral character. Deep disagreement exists, however, over what should be in third place on that list of qualifications. One group of pastors insists it should be effective service as the senior minister of a very large congregation. Others place that no higher than tenth or twentieth on their list of desirable qualities.

In recent times the actions and public statements of American bishops, archbishops, and cardinals of the Roman Catholic Church have provided millions of column inches of reporting for newspapers and news magazines. The episcopal system also has provided millions of dollars in income for tort lawyers over the past quarter century.

By contrast, many of the contented members of those American nondenominational megachurches who date the beginning of the contemporary Christian era with the founding of their congregation in 1975 or 1998 regard this as a nonissue. They are more likely to focus their attention on how to reach bored or disillusioned Christians who have dropped out of church or on the location of the coffee bar and food court in their new building or on organizing additional adult Bible fellowships.

The episcopal polity appears to be appropriate and effective in several institutional environments. These include an ecclesiastical environment that (a) is organized around certainty, not ambiguity and/or (b) calls for members to perceive this as a lifelong commitment to a high commitment covenant community and/or (c) is NOT interested in being an active participant in a movement for Christian unity with religious traditions that do not have an episcopal polity and/or (d) organizes its midlevel judicatories on the principle that affiliated congregations will be similar in size, type, and role and/or (e) includes very few congregations averaging more than 350 at worship and/or (f) calls for clearly defined and very high standards of personal behavior among the members and/or (g) does NOT place a high value on egalitarianism, individual self-determination, participatory democracy, demographic diversity, or ideological pluralism and/or (h) is designed with a hierarchical organizational structure and/or (i) chooses bishops for life rather than for a defined term of office and/or (j) places a high value on "taking good care" of the clergy and/or (k) operates on the assumption that denominations, not congregations, are the primary channels for fulfilling the Great Commission and also are basic building blocks for interchurch cooperation and/or (l) chooses congregational leaders, both lay and clergy, who affirm and accept the authority of distant leaders and recognize the limited wisdom of local leaders and/or (m) places the greatest emphasis in worship and teaching on God the Creator rather than on the second or third persons of the Holy Trinity and/or (n) places a higher value on taking good care of today's members and a lower value on evangelism and/or (o) perhaps most critical of all, operates on the assumption tradition should be more influential than the Great Commission in determining the priorities in the allocation of scarce resources.

Those Christian traditions in America that display a least nine of those fourteen characteristics sshould be able to continue with an episcopal polity for many more generations into the future.

For those strongly committed to perpetuating the office of bishop, there appears to be three promising alternatives. One is to adapt the Asian-Christian and the African American model and (a) reduce the workload largely to ceremonial duties and (b) make the job a part-time assignment for a parish pastor.

A second alternative is to adapt the Western European-American model being used by an increasing number of college and university presidents as well as bishops. This calls for approximately 20 percent of the bishop's time and energy to be devoted to ceremonial duties; 50 percent to soliciting contributions from individuals, family foundations, larger foundations, corporations, governmental agencies, and social entrepreneurs for funding the current budget of that judicatory and for congregational needs; 15 percent to increasing the endowment fund of that judicatory; and 15 percent to administrative and teaching duties. Since this requires building long-term relationships with potential contributors, the tenure of the bishop should be in the fifteen- to thirty-year range. A reasonable goal is that by year five of a bishop's tenure at least one-half of the expenditures of that diocese, synod, conference, or district will be funded by these gifts.[4]

The third, and by far the most difficult, alternative is for the bishop to accept the role of a transformational leader. This usually means replacing the old ecclesiastical system based on tradition, rules, and a hierarchical organizational structure with a new system designed to help congregations focus on the transformation of lives as they seek to fulfill the Great Commission. This calls for pumping water up a very steep hill!

In other words, don't underestimate the power of tradition in nonprofit institutions!

The last third of the twentieth century clearly brought significant changes, in terms of polity, to the American ecclesiastical scene. The absence of consistency in those trends does raise a question about the future. The move of the Southern Baptist Convention toward a Baptist adaptation of the presbyterian system is a move in one direction. The possible recognition of ministerial standing of clergy from other traditions in the emerging coalition that includes the Episcopal Church, the Lutheran Church in America, the Presbyterian Church (U.S.A.), the United Church of Christ, the Reformed Church in America, and the Moravian Church in America could evolve into a major step toward Christian unity despite huge differences in polity and doctrine.

In both the Roman Catholic Church in America and The United Methodist Church recent decades have brought an expansion in the staff assigned to the office of bishop as part of a larger effort to strengthen the episcopal system. Instead of allocating scarce financial resources to new church development, the decision was made to allocate those dollars to strengthening the episcopal system.

Rather than look back and attempt to identify recent trends and predict the future from the past, it may be more productive to begin with a blank sheet of paper and ask the question, "What would be the best polity for a religious tradition in twenty-first century America?" Before going down that trail, however, it is necessary to chase one more rabbit.

What Happened to the Presbyterian System?

Few will quarrel with these three broad generalizations.

First, the level of complexity in the American economy and culture today is far greater than it was in 1940. That generalization applies to agriculture, mining, transportation, retail trade, cameras, communications, education, the practice of law, the practice of medicine, and the practice of ministry.

Second, the differences among people, goods, and institutions are far greater than ever before. That generalization applies to motor vehicles, farms, motion picture theaters, high schools, single family homes, shoes, aircraft, financial institutions, television stations, housing for the elderly, professional athletes, universities, and Christian congregations.

Third, it is increasingly difficult to design one system to produce a service that meets the needs of all potential constituents. That generalization applies to elementary schools, restaurants, clothes, hospitals, motor vehicles, computers, medical prescriptions, greeting cards, newspapers, television programs, hotels and motels, bicycles, churches, tractors, and the midlevel judicatories in American Christianity. The demand is for "a customized design that fits my needs."

Add those three generalizations together, and we have one explanation for the problems confronting the presbyterian system of church government. When it was imported to America from

Europe, a persuasive argument could be made that the presbyterian system of church government was the ideal system for Protestant Christians pioneering a new world. It is a representative democracy, rather than the participatory democracy of pure congregationalism, it is built on the power of peer relationships, affirms the merits of appeals, and places a high value on the interdependence of congregations.

What happened? For obvious reasons the midlevel judicatories in the presbyterian systems were defined in geographical terms. The combination of the limitations of transportation and communication plus a relatively high degree of homogeneity among the congregations and clergy made that both necessary and feasible. In recent decades the three trends described here have undercut the feasibility of the geographically defined midlevel judiatory.

Does the presbyterian system of polity have a future?

Certainly!

Three modest changes, however, will be required to accomplish that. One is to decrease the emphasis on the regulatory role.[5] The number of American Christians who want to be regulated is now smaller than the number who want to regulate the beliefs, behavior, and practices of others. Second, the most effective midlevel judicatories in the presbyterian system will be those that enjoy a high degree of homogeneity among the affiliated congregations in terms of ideology, role, goals, definition of congregational priorities, type, size, community environment, pastoral leadership, and dreams. Third, that emphasis on a regulatory role must be replaced by a self-defined role as helping congregations fulfill the Great Commission.

What Is the Best Polity?

If you are a professional scout for a major league baseball team, you will always be eager to discover that tall, slender, left-handed teenager who possesses the gift of a natural fastball that registers ninety-eight miles per hour on your speed gun. You are looking for a scarce and valuable talent, and you begin with several crite-ria, left-handed, young, tall, natural fastball, and slender.

What is the best polity for an American Protestant denomina-tion in the twenty-first century? A good beginning point is crite-ria. This observer brings a dozen to the table.

1. Polity should be seen as a means-to-an-end, not as an end in itself. What is the best polity for a Protestant denomination in America in the twenty-first century? The polity that will be most useful in enabling that denomination to achieve its goals. This book focuses on the midlevel judicatory. Therefore the best polity is the one that will enable that midlevel judicatory to fulfill its number-one reason for existing.

2. The central theme of this book is midlevel judicatories exist primarily to help congregations fulfill the Great Commission. Therefore the polity should be designed to help congregational leaders fulfill the Great Commission. It should not be designed primarily around the care of the clergy or the redistribution of income and wealth or a regulatory role or the promotion of Christian unity or perpetuating old traditions unless that has been defined as the number-one item on the agenda of that midlevel judicatory.

3. The New Testament places a far greater emphasis on the interdependence of the churches than on absolute autonomy. This is a recurring theme in the letters of Paul. Therefore the best polity should affirm the interdependence of congregations.

4. The design should not be driven by distrust of the laity in general and local (congregational) leadership in particular, but rather by a conviction that the laity can be trusted and if chal-lenged, equipped to help fulfill the Great Commission. They will respond when properly challenged and nurtured and also benefit personally and spiritually.

5. The doctrine of original sin is real and no sinful human being is perfect. Therefore every congregation will benefit from being part of an ecclesiastical system based on the interdepen-dence of congregations, the oversight of peers, and an affirmation of the right to appeal that first decision.

The appeal of what is perceived to be a wrong decision to an impartial outside third party has become a firmly established right of the American legal system and the contemporary American culture. That right can be a positive component of a healthy system of governance in American Christianity.

(This may be the most divisive statement in this book. Tens of thousands of adult American Christians disagree. They contend that right of appeal does and should exist, but ends with the congregational meeting. The elders of that church are authorized to make all decisions on all matters. If and when a member disagrees with that decision, the right of appeal is to a congregational meeting. That decision is final! Complete congregational autonomy does not allow any appeal to any "outside" third party, either civil or religious. This may be the most significant fork-in-the-road-to-tomorrow issue raised in this book. My contention is this is a doctrine of original sin issue and should be considered in light of that doctrine as well as the next statement.)

6. During the first third of the nineteenth century American Protestants finally accepted the concept that the Christian church in the United States is a voluntary association. A central characteristic of a voluntary association is every member retains the right to withdraw. The United States Army is NOT a voluntary association![6]

Should an American Protestant congregation offer members the unilateral right to withdraw their membership? Should an American Protestant denomination offer congregations the right of unilateral withdrawal, perhaps only with a sixty-to-forty or seventy-to-thirty vote?

Is this a Roman Catholic-American Protestant line of demarcation? Most American Protestant denominations perceive themselves to be voluntary associations and the unilateral right of congregations to withdraw is accepted without serious ideological debate.

If the denomination is a self-identified covenant community, withdrawal is possible only by approval of the majority of peers. If the denomination is a self-identified voluntary association, unilateral withdrawal is a part of the definition. Do you believe your denomination displays the basic characteristics of a covenant community with universal agreement on doctrine, role, values, goals, priorities in ministry, and criteria for membership? Or do you believe your denomination more closely resembles a voluntary association under a broad umbrella that affirms diversity, pluralism, and self-determination?

Any effort to encourage diversity, pluralism, and self-determination in a self-identified covenant community with a very high threshold into membership is guaranteed to produce either a highly centralized authoritarian dictatorship or internal conflict, alienation, and disorder.

7. The design of the polity should be driven by helping congregations enhance their capability to fulfill the Great Commission rather than to perpetuate old institutional traditions.

This should be recognized as a highly controversial statement. My travels have led me to listen to scores of deeply committed Christians who are completely convinced the number-one frontier in fulfilling the Great Commission is their denomination. Congregations should resource the denomination in accomplishing its mission and the polity should be designed to facilitate that process. This statement advocates a polity designed to facilitate denominational agencies in helping congregations fulfill the Great Commission. Which is the number-one frontier in mission in twenty-first century America? Congregations or denominational agencies?

8. Experience suggests the denominational polity can be used to create highly disruptive adversarial relationships between congregational leaders and denominational leaders. To some degree this goes back to the old conflict between master and servant. Does the master evaluate the performance of the servant? Certainly! Does the servant evaluate the master? Certainly! Conflict and alienation can be reduced if the polity provides absolute clarity on (a) the identification of the master and the identification of the servant and (b) the criteria each will use in the evaluation of the other.

Does the polity of your denomination assume a servant role for congregations and a "master knows best" role for denominational agencies? Or does it begin with the assumption that denominational agencies exist to help congregations—a servant role—fulfill the Great Commission?

After every leader agrees on the same answer to those two questions, it will be appropriate to move the discussion to the next five questions.

What are the criteria congregations in your denomination should use in evaluating the performance of denominational agencies in general and the performance of the midlevel judicatories in particular? What are the appropriate criteria for denominational leaders to use in evaluating the ministry of congregations? Is there widespread agreement by both parties on both sets of criteria? Should an annual performance audit be a part of that evaluation process? Does the polity encourage clarity or ambiguity on those questions?

9. From this observer's perspective one of the most important criteria is the polity should be designed to encourage congregational leaders to learn from leaders in other churches how to fulfill the Great Commission and to carry out other ministries effectively. Does your current polity facilitate that?

10. A related crucial assumption is Congregation A can benefit the most by learning from Congregation B when five or ten years earlier Congregation B closely resembled contemporary reality at Congregation A and today Congregation B closely resembles what God is calling Congregation A to be and to be doing in the years ahead.

In other words, learn from others who are traveling down the same road you are traveling and especially those who are ahead of you in their pilgrimage.

11. A common practice in America is for a child to enroll in elementary school, graduate a few years later, move to a new pedagogical environment called a middle school or junior high school, graduate, move to a new and more challenging learning environment called a high school, graduate, and move to a new learning environment called a college or a university. Once in awhile an adult may resign from one job to take a new position

in a more challenging vocational setting. It is not uncommon for Christians to reflect on their personal faith pilgrimage as they moved from agnostic to seeker to new believer to eager learner to disciple to deeply committed apostle. Every week scores of mature adults who have spent several decades in the Frostbelt retire to begin a new chapter of their life in the Sunbelt.

Is it reasonable to assume that in a similar pattern Christian congregations may advance from one chapter of their history to write a new chapter? For example, at least a few American Protestant congregations began their history as small neighborhood churches in a rural farming community. As the cornfields began to be replaced with single-family homes, shopping centers, office buildings, parking lots, new public schools, and recreational facilities, some of these churches became exurban congregations. A decade or two later a few became very large regional churches. An equal number either dissolved or merged with another small church.

Another congregation was founded as a German language neighborhood church in 1890. By 1915 it had been transformed into a bilingual parish and by 1945 it was an English-language congregation. In 1960, following racial changes in the population, it relocated to become a white suburban neighborhood church. In 1975 the congregation purchased adjacent land and today it is a large predominantly Anglo regional church.

As it moves from one stage of its history into a new and different stage, should a congregation continue to be a member of the same midlevel judicatory? Or should it be enabled, and perhaps even encouraged, to transfer its affiliation to a midlevel judicatory better equipped to resource its ministry plan for a new tomorrow?

If one switches the focus from congregations to church buildings, the answer is clearly in the affirmative, but with one reservation. That reservation is any switch in midlevel judicatories usually is accompanied by a change in denominational affiliation. That building now housing a Baptist congregation was constructed by a Roman Catholic parish in 1903. That building housing a United Methodist congregation was built by a

Universalist Church in 1880. That structure housing a Pentecostal church was constructed in 1912 by a Swedish Lutheran parish. That huge structure erected by a Reformed Church now houses an independent congregation.

The operational rule appears to be for church buildings to be able to switch their regional judicatories, they must leave their original denomination.

We also can find thousands of Protestant congregations that have switched their midlevel judicatory affiliation, but most had to switch denominational affiliation or do it through a denominational reorganization.

A more lenient policy applies to pastors. Tens of thousands have switched from one midlevel judicatory to another, but continued their same denominational ties.

This raises a fundamental policy issue. If a congregation wants to switch from one midlevel judicatory to one with which it has a greater degree of compatibility, must it also switch denominations? Or can it do that and retain its denominational affiliation? Currently this is a highly divisive issue in the Southern Baptist Convention and is beginning to surface in other denominations.

This introduces what some readers may conclude is a revolutionary concept. From this observer's perspective the ideal polity will make it easy for congregations to switch their affiliation from one midlevel judicatory to another within that same denominational family. Instead of encouraging members, the clergy, and congregations to depart for another denomination, encourage them to remain within that larger denominational family!

This concept could be expanded to REQUIRE that every fifth (third?) year every congregation will decide to continue or to switch its midlevel judicatory affiliation. One way to improve the performance of any organization is to enhance its sensitivity to the customer's expectations. (This criterion, of course, is completely irrelevant if the design of the polity calls for congregations to make their top priority resourcing the needs of the denomination!)

12. Finally, the ideal polity will be designed to minimize diversionary and divisive internal quarrels that distract from an

emphasis on fulfilling the Great Commission. The greater the degree of ideological pluralism and/or demographic diversity, the easier it is to divert time and energy to highly divisive issues. Throughout the history of the Christian churches, the number-one temptation has been to quarrel over sex and gender issues.

One response, modeled by the Christian Reformed Church in North America, has been to keep at least a few of these issues off the agenda of the national church and refer them to the regional judicatories. Let each regional judicatory decide where it stands, for example, on the issue of the ordination of women.

The next step, which is a central theme of this book, is to create nongeographical and homogeneous midlevel judicatories. Each congregation could choose the midlevel judicatory on the basis of "That's where we belong." That is the identical criterion used by many churchgoers born after 1970 in choosing a church home.

One possible reservation would be an open door to any congregation seeking to join a geographically defined midlevel judicatory if that congregation met in a building within the boundaries of that judicatory, but a majority vote of approval from member churches would be required for any congregation asking for membership in an affinity judicatory.

In summary, how do we create a polity for our denomination that (a) makes it easier for everyone to focus on the call to fulfill the Great Commission, (b) accommodates a relatively high level of demographic diversity, (c) affirms at least a moderate degree of ideological pluralism, (d) increases the probability of a good match when a congregation searches for a new pastor to succeed the departing minister, (e) minimizes internal diversionary quarrels, (f) strengthens the loyalty of congregations to our denomination, and (g) affirms the creativity, initiative, vision, competence, and commitment of congregational leaders?

A response to that question requires a more detailed discussion of affinity networks and judicatories, but, before exploring that subject, let us take a detour, thanks to my friend, Tom Ambler, to discover what can be learned from the theater.

WHAT IS YOUR FRAME OF REFERENCE?

The weather forecast advises that tomorrow's high temperature will be 60 degrees on the Fahrenheit scale. How do you respond to that? If today is July in Tucson, that is good, but perhaps unbelievable news. If today is January in Montana, that also is hard to believe. If today is April in Ohio, that is about what we hoped to hear.

Everyone of us carries a frame of reference in our head that guides our thinking as we are introduced to a new idea.

What is the frame of reference that guides your thinking when you consider how and why adult social networks are formed? Is the key variable age or language or place of birth or ancestry or place of residence or formal education or church affiliation or occupation or skin color or place of work or hobbies or marital status or gender or income or military service or social class or kinship ties or music or travel or some other point of commonality?

What is the key variable in your frame of reference as you reflect on what would be the ideal organizational structure for your denomination? Is it geography or tradition or the convenience of denominational officials or fulfilling the Great Commission or taking better care of pastors or minimizing expenditures or the differences in religious cultures or the ministerial placement process or the easiest way to raise money or promoting social justice or advancing Christian unity or strengthening the Sunday school or some other priority or goal?

What is a useful frame of reference to guide your thinking as you reflect on the possibility of offering the congregations in your denomination a choice between affiliation with a midlevel regional judicatory based on geographically defined boundaries or a nongeographical affinity judicatory? One possibility is to look at three kinds of theater.

This is not a new idea! In August 1988 George Plagenz, the religion editor for the *Cleveland Plain Dealer*, wrote a nationally syndicated article, "Pulpit Must Be Good Theater." Plagenz argued that good preaching, like good theater, requires passion, conviction, thought, feeling, and a central theme. Good theater "must be stimulating to the ear, the eye and the mind of the members of the audience," wrote Plagenz.

Three Types of Theater

One contemporary facet of American life is called "street theater." This often takes the form of protests by the self-identified advocates of reform who are attacking those in power. It may include marches, signs, pantomime, slogans, pickets, music, loudspeakers, costumes, and other expressions of protests against the status quo. The recipients of these messages usually are identified as people who are abusing the power of their office. That long list includes employers, governmental officials, officers of international corporations, manufacturers, religious leaders, and other oppressors of the powerless.

Street theater is marked by passion, conviction, emotion, and a central theme. That central theme is opposition to perpetuating the status quo. It may not include a detailed strategy for reform.

The street theater model has been and continues to be widely used by ad hoc groups protesting the policies and actions of both Protestant and Roman Catholic organizations and leaders. Street theater usually rallies supporters on the basis of either *"what* we oppose" or *"who* we oppose." Frequently the players in street theater have not achieved detailed and broad-based support for a specific course of action. Participants agree on the identity of the enemy, but they may not agree on the terms of a peace treaty.

A second, and far more common, type of theater is the traditional stage play. The performers may be eighth graders or college students or professional actors and actresses. The play may be presented in a high school auditorium or in the fellowship hall of a church or in a professional theater. As Rosabeth Moss Kanter has pointed out in an exceptionally provocative essay, most stage plays display the same characteristics.[1] The play is carefully scripted. The performers are chosen to match the roles in the script. They memorize their parts. They rehearse repeatedly. Finally, after a huge investment of time and energy, the day of the first performance arrives. All the cast knows exactly what the final ending will be. Each time that play is presented, it follows that predetermined course with exactly the same conclusion. Occasionally one of the performers must be replaced, but that newcomer is expected to memorize the part and fit into that carefully scripted role.

Predictability, quality, performance, control, repetition, and following the script are among the desired characteristics of traditional theater. A parallel in large Protestant churches is the pastor who reads the identical sermon, word for word, at three worship services on Sunday morning or the chancel choir who present the same anthem two or three times every Sunday morning.

The typical geographically defined regional judicatory in American Protestantism usually resembles the carefully scripted traditional theater. That script may have been written by an earlier generation of policymakers. It may have been written several generations ago by what are now referred to as dead white males, but who were influential policymakers when they were alive. It may have been written by national denominational officials who act on the assumption the regional leadership cannot be trusted and therefore require a script in order to act. That script for the regional actors may have been written by those who were convinced the central theme should be to perpetuate the past or to service the agendas of the national agencies of that denomination.

Whether they be paid staff members or volunteers serving on boards and committees, the actors in that geographically defined regional judicatory rarely gather around a table with nothing on it. The script for that particular act in that play already has been written, and a copy is at each participant's place at the table. Frequently the script includes an agenda, a rulebook, a calendar, a budget, and a list of influential precedents, sometimes referred to as "the minutes of our last meeting."

Several actors in the play performed by the actors in that geographically defined regional judicatory will be in the same location and follow a similar script to when that act was performed a year ago or a decade earlier. Several of the actors from the particular act in the play in three earlier performances will have been replaced, but the script is the same, and the outcome is predictable.

In her research on how profit-driven companies respond to technological change, Professor Kanter discovered the most effective "tended to act before they had a complete plan" in place. They empowered innovators, expected the employees to be creative and to improvise, were able to adjust to unanticipated needs of their customers, and involved more people. They created the plan as they responded to the need for change. Instead of waiting for those in charge to create the perfect plan, these organizations placed a high level of trust in those responsible for carrying out the plan.

Professor Kanter compares this to what is often described as improvisational theater. This third form of theater does not depend on a script prepared in advance. It trusts the actors to be unpredictable, to innovate, and to be comfortable helping to create the action. A crucial point in the success of improvisational theater is it must be driven by a single theme that also stimulates spontaneity, opens the door to serendipity, encourages creativity, and expects participants to "think outside the box," and try the untested.

Improvisational theater demands far more of the actors than does the traditional scripted play. They must be comfortable with the unexpected, quick on their feet, able to come up with an appropriate response to surprises, and enjoy suspense. Traditional theater serves one audience at a time, all in one room. Improvisational theater is able to adjust to a variety of responses from several different audiences in a variety of settings.

The New Wineskins Thesis

The most memorable sentence in Professor Kanter's essay declares, "You can't create the future in a structure designed to repeat the past."

That statement explains why this book recommends the creation of new affinity judicatories rather than suggestions on how to reform existing systems.

What is the theme? Every form of theater, whether it be street, traditional, or improvisational, requires a central theme. In the ideal world the central theme of every affinity judicatory will be the same. We exist to help congregations fulfill the Great Commission. As was pointed out earlier, this is not a new idea! Working models are in operation in the Texas Diocese of the Episcopal Church, among the Southern Baptists in South Carolina, and other places.

If a major goal is to open the door wider so the power of the Holy Spirit may direct the renewal of your denominational system, the improvisational theater model may be a way to accomplish that.

A supplemental theme reinforces that central theme. Each affinity judicatory is organized to enhance the capability of congregational leaders to learn from one another. The congregations in any one affinity judicatory share several points of commonality. These could include (a) the definition of our primary constituency, (b) size, (c) community context, (d) congregational culture, (e) staff configuration, (f) distinctive role, (g) race, language, or ancestry, (h) theological stance, (i) partners in local ministry, (j) stance on issue-centered ministries, (k) real estate, or (l) the design of corporate worship experiences.

Where do we look for a model of this organizational structure? One alternative filled with relevant insights and warning signs is theater. That also could be your frame of reference for reading the next chapter.

WHAT IS AN AFFINITY JUDICATORY?

The concept of a nongeographically defined affinity conference or district or synod or midlevel judicatory is far from a new idea. The nongeographical English District of the Lutheran Church-Missouri Synod traces its history back to 1911.

It was created to serve those Lutheran parishes that preferred English to German as the language for worship and for transmitting the Christian faith to the next generation.

As recently as 1906 the Methodist Episcopal Church included nine German conferences, four Swedish conferences, two Spanish conferences, and one Danish conference as well as a dozen missionary conferences. Currently at least two dozen American Protestant denominations include midlevel judicatories that are defined in terms of affinity rather than geography.

Perhaps the most common examples of the affinity judicatory among the predominantly white and English-speaking American Protestant denominations are those designed for an immigrant constituency such as the Swedish Methodist Conference or the Slovak Synod or the Korean Presbytery or the Chinese District. This is an especially attractive system for those denominations that (a) have been actively engaged in planting new missions on other continents and (b) are actively seeking to reach and serve recent immigrants from the Pacific Rim, Latin America, and other parts of the world. The Christian and Missionary Alliance with a dozen affinity districts stands out as an exemplary model of this strategy.

These immigrant church judicatories illustrate two of the key assumptions behind the creation of affinity groups. The first is to bring people together around a meaningful point of commonality and to affirm that point of commonality. The church growth movement has coined the term "homogeneous unit principle" to describe this concept. The jocks in high school tend to socialize with one another. Back in that era when colleges and universities had single-sex dormitories, dorm loyalty was one effort to socialize eighteen-year-olds into a new affinity group. Basic training was designed to socialize new recruits into a military organization. Swedish Lutheran parishes were founded in communities with a large German Lutheran population to welcome and assimilate newcomers from Sweden.

The second assumption behind the creation of affinity groups is that central organizing principle is not expected to last forever. As the years roll by, that seventeen-year-old star quarterback eventually becomes a high school teacher, a husband, a father, and a grandfather. He looks for new affinity groups at each stage of life. The Evangelical Lutheran Church in America is the successor to what once were nearly a dozen different monocultural affinity denominations.

One moral of those two paragraphs is that it should be relatively easy for a congregation to identify with two networks concurrently. For example, the Willow Creek Association, which is an outstanding example of a new affinity network, includes many congregations that also are affiliated with a mainline Protestant denomination. Multitasking affirms a person's right to read the newspaper while eating breakfast or to listen to music while operating a computer or to operate a motor vehicle while concurrently talking on a cell phone and scaring pedestrians. Likewise a congregation can be a full member of a geographically defined regional judicatory while concurrently enjoying the benefits of membership in an affinity judicatory.

The second moral of this story is to keep open the door to the future. Since 1950 tens of thousands of American Protestant congregations have changed their affiliation with a geographically defined synod, diocese, region, district, conference, or presbytery while continuing to meet at the same address. Denominational mergers and restructuring efforts have demonstrated that a congregation's tie to one particular regional judicatory is like marriage, it may or may not be a long-term relationship.

What Is the Question?

Before moving on to illustrate the variety of affinity networks and a discussion of why the new ecclesiastical economy encourages the creation of affinity networks and affinity judicatories, it may be useful to state the question. The issue is NOT do you favor congregations turning to affinity networks as they seek help in learning how to do ministry in the twenty-first century! Thousands of congregations already are doing that, and that number increases weekly.

The real question is do you favor congregations turning to (a) affinity networks that are not related to your denomination as they seek help or (b) affinity networks within your denominational system as they seek help? The record to date is clear on four counts.

1. More and more congregations are seeking help as they design a customized ministry plan for their future in what is clearly an increasingly competitive ecclesiastical economy.

2. The more relevant and useful is the help they receive, the greater their sense of allegiance to the source of that help.

3. If their denominational system does not offer the relevant and quality help they desire, many congregations are ready to go outside their system for resources.

4. Perceived irrelevance is a guaranteed route to undermining loyalty to institutions. That generalization applies to political parties, governmental agencies, health care systems, educational institutions, religious bodies, youth groups, labor unions, retail stores, and publishing houses.

As you design your denominational system for the twenty-first century, do you prefer to reinforce or undermine the loyalty of affiliated congregations to your denomination? That is a fringe benefit issue, not a central organizing principle, but it should not be ignored.

Which One Is for You?

Could your congregation benefit from belonging to an affinity network or an affinity-based judicatory? A common answer is, "No, unless we can find one that matches the culture, ideological position, purpose, role, distinctive personality, type, or aspirations of our congregation." An affirmative response by a majority of congregations to that question will require their being able to choose from among a large array of options. It is easy to offer a list of forty-four actual or potential affinity networks to illustrate that range of possibilities.

1. The monocultural network or judicatory for congregations consisting largely of adults who were born in the same foreign country and were adults when they emigrated to the United States.

2. Ditto, but for congregations consisting largely of adults born in another country who came to the United States as children and were reared in an immigrant family but educated in the American public school system.

3. Ditto, but for congregations consisting largely of adults who were born in America to parents of a foreign ancestry.

4. The network or judicatory of congregations including large numbers of couples in an intercultural marriage. This may require at least four different networks—Asian-Anglo, Hispanic-Anglo, Black-Anglo, and Black-Hispanic.

5. The network for congregations that share one full-time pastor with one or two other churches.

6. The network of congregations served by a part-time pastor who concurrently is a seminary student.

7. The network for "Old First Church" downtown type congregations averaging at least seven hundred at worship.

8. The network for churches with a Christian day school for ages four through at least eight or nine.

9. The network for multisite congregations.

10. The network for congregations focused on reaching and serving young adults in the twenty-five to thirty-five age bracket, both never married and childless couples.

11. The network for self-identified "University Churches." (This is one of the two or three most demanding and sophisticated specialized roles on the contemporary church scene.)

12. The network for congregations organized as a collection of high expectation learning communities.

13. The network of congregations served by a dual career minister with one career as a part-time pastor and the other career as a homemaker.

14. The network of congregations served by a dual career minister with full-time secular employment who also is a part-time parish pastor.

15. The network for those congregations that are affiliated with a denomination that is NOT one of the historic "peace churches" (Friends, Brethren, Mennonite), but self-identified classical pacifists constitute their primary constituency.

16. A network of congregations organized around alleviating world hunger as their central organizing principle.

17. A network of congregations that own and operate one or more specialized housing ventures (for the developmentally

disabled or transitional housing for single-parent mothers or for retirees or for the physically disabled or for the homeless or for political refugees).

18. A network for self-identified teaching churches that do NOT include an on-campus classroom program leading to a master's degree.

19. A network of self-identified teaching churches that do offer the classroom experiences required for an accredited master's degree.

20. A network of congregations with an affiliated foundation with assets in excess of $10 million.

21. A network for new missions founded within the previous three years including new missions about to be launched.

22. A network for small rural congregations with persons working in agriculture as their primary constituency.

23. A network for nonmetropolitan churches with retirees as their primary constituency.

24. A network for nonmetropolitan churches with persons commuting to an urban job as their primary constituency.

25. A network for nonmetropolitan churches with workers and guests in the recreation and entertainment industry as their primary constituency.

26. A network for nonmetropolitan churches that are responding to the change from rural to exurban in the local economy and culture.

27. A network for five-to-ten-year-old new missions that have plateaued in size with an average worship attendance in the 125-to-250 range.

28. A network for congregations averaging 125-to-350 at worship and located in a rural county seat community with a population in the 2,500-to-10,000 bracket.

29. A network for self-identified "seeker-sensitive" churches that focus on adult nonbelievers as their primary constituency.

30. A network for congregations who have identified Christian believers who do not have any active church relationship as their primary constituency. (Any denomination that defines self-identified Christian believers who have become disillusioned

with what they perceive to be the "traditional institutional expression" of Christianity as their primary unchurched constituency to be reached by that denomination probably should (a) launch at least one hundred new missions annually to reach this large slice of the American population and (b) create at least five or six nongeographical affinity judicatories to serve these new missions and the existing congregations that describe this population as their primary constituency.)

31. A network for churches that have accepted as their distinctive role helping believers (both new and long time) become well informed and deeply committed believers.

32. A network for congregations that have accepted as their distinctive role challenging and enabling believers to become fully devoted disciples of Jesus Christ.

33. A network for high-expectation congregations that have decided to challenge disciples to be engaged in those transformational life-changing experiences that transform believers and disciples into apostles engaged in doing ministry.

34. A network for churches that schedule a traditional liturgical worship organized around Holy Communion every week with a homily, a vocal choir, and organ music as the principal worship service of the week, and this is the only or at least the most well-attended service of the week.

35. A network for congregations that have identified as their primary source of adult new members persons who were reared in the Roman Catholic Church, have become discontented or disillusioned with the Catholic Church in America, and are seeking a more compatible church home. (See chapter 2.)

36. One of the most interesting new affinity networks is organized with a Christian college at the hub and a voluntary relationship with several score or a few hundred congregations. The primary agenda can be condensed into three questions, (1) How can this Christian college resource these congregations? (2) How can these congregations resource the college? (3) How can this network help these churches resource one another?

37. A distinctive network could consist of those congregations that have decided to resource home-schooling families.

38. A great need could be filled by creating an affinity network to resource those congregations that have assembled and trained teams of volunteers who serve as advocates for those people who need assistance in dealing with the complicated bureaucratic systems of the current American economy. These advocates include social workers, retired bureaucrats, teachers, physicians, attorneys, pharmacists, parish nurses, counselors, paralegal specialists, and financial planners.

39. One of the most urgently needed networks could be for congregations that have decided to compete with night school classes, bars, park district programs, newspaper ads, and restaurants. What is the point of commonality? Where does the single twenty-eight-year-old or thirty-seven-year-old or sixty-one-year-old go to meet a potential future spouse who shares a Christian value system? Several dozen congregations have decided to help fill that vacuum, but they could benefit by (a) learning from one another and (b) cooperating in offering regional events bringing together single adults from two dozen Christian congregations.

40. A new affinity network could be of value to those congregations that enlist teams of seven-to-fifteen volunteers to go as short-term missionaries and work with members of a sister church on another continent.

41. Long overdue is the affinity network that will bring together the full-time media specialists from a few dozen congregations that create videotapes to be used in worship, in teaching, and in community outreach and are made available to other churches.

42. Several affinity networks are needed for those congregations that have decided to give a high priority to helping engaged couples and newlyweds discover how to build a healthy, happy, and enduring marriage. (A persuasive argument can be made that this should be at the top of this list of needed networks.)

43. An obvious need is for the affinity judicatory to resource congregations that believe they are called by God to become multicultural (that is far more difficult than bicultural) worshiping communities in which no one ethnic or cultural or nationality group constitutes more than one-third of the constituency and

that also are self-governing, self-expressing, self-financing, and self-propagating congregations. This is near the top of that list of how congregations can benefit from learning from the experiences of others.

44. For those denominations seriously interested in reaching American-born adults under age fifty, the largest affinity judicatories could be those designed to resource the new wave of house churches. These lay-led worshiping communities typically include seven-to-thirty-five people. This is consistent with contemporary reality in several denominations in which the most frequently cited numbers in reporting average worship attendance are twenty, twenty-five, thirty, thirty-five, and forty.

Among the most highly visible differences between the current generation of house churches and the typical small congregation are (a) they are lay-led and not dependent on clergy leadership, (b) they do not own any real estate, (c) somewhere between 70 and 100 percent of their financial receipts are allocated to benevolent causes, (d) the Sunday (or Saturday evening) schedule usually includes worship, learning, a meal, fellowship, and a strong emphasis on the power of intercessory prayer, (e) many also serve as a mutual support group, (f) instead of being sent off to Sunday school, the family atmosphere encourages children to be a part of that gathered worshiping community, and (g) the size, the sense of community, and the ease of assimilation make these attractive entry points for younger adults on a self-identified religious pilgrimage and for those who have been turned off by the traditional institutional expression of the Christian church or those who place a high value on community.

How easy is it for a first-time visitor to gain a sense of belonging in a house church? Several alternatives stand out, (a) offer to host next week's gathering in your home, (b) come early next week to help prepare the meal, (c) stay late this week to visit and help with the cleanup, (d) accept a speaking or leadership role in next week's worship experience or time for teaching, (e) share your story and your joys and concerns during that period of intercessory prayer, (f) be invited by a friend who is a member, or (g) help staff a new outreach task force.

A reasonable estimate is that any American Protestant denomination that (a) is interested in creating and nurturing one or more networks of house churches and (b) is willing to learn from the experiences of others could include hundreds of affiliated house churches within a decade. A modest goal could be for every current affiliated congregation averaging 125 or more at worship, by 2012 the roster of affiliated congregations also could include three or four house churches.

Why not encourage these small lay-led independent worshiping communities to affiliate with a geographically defined regional judicatory where they could learn how to double or triple or quadruple in size? First of all, affiliation with a regional judicatory is not necessarily the road to numerical growth. More important, however, is the agenda of these lay-led worshiping communities has very little overlap with clergy-led congregations in which one-half to three-fourths of the expenditures are allocated to care of the real estate and staff compensation.

Among the best places to look for contemporary models of these small, nondenominational, and lay-led worshiping communities that do not own or rent real estate are (a) on other continents, (b) among the immigrant congregations in the United States, (c) in retirement communities, (d) on college and university campuses, (e) in large office buildings housing scores of white collar employees, and (f) in prisons and jails.

A better beginning point should be to ask why any of these nondenominational small lay-led worshiping communities would choose to affiliate with an established denomination? Why not create their own fellowship of house churches?

One motivation could be a desire to be connected with the larger church. A second could be more opportunities to give, to share, to support other ministries and, perhaps most attractive of all, to be involved in doing ministry with fellow Christians. Few of these small worshiping communities can mobilize the resources required to be engaged in ministry with a sister church on another continent that calls for American volunteers to spend ten-to-fifteen days once or twice a year as short-term missionaries with fellow Christians in Latin America or Asia or Eastern Europe. Few are able to offer parishioners the option of a Christian day school or a youth ministry including three dozen teenagers or a class for newlyweds on how to build a healthy, happy, and enduring marriage. A denominational tie would make it easier to offer more choices to the constituency of that small lay-led worshiping community.

The denominational system could be redesigned to provide a variety of meaningful and memorable experiences, learning opportunities, and choices to be engaged in doing ministry to those who prefer the intimacy, the sense of community, the scale, and the self-determination of that small worshiping community. One of these would be to learn from one another. The nongeographically defined judicatory consisting only of these congregations also could be a valuable learning resource for traditional congregations.

This could be a logical component of a larger strategy for those denominations that have placed a high priority on the ministry of the small church. The United Methodist Church, for example, includes nearly 6,500 congregations that report an average worship attendance of twenty-five or fewer. Most of these allocate a substantial proportion of their resources to maintaining a meeting place.

A reasonable United Methodist goal, for example, would be to invite several thousand existing nondenominational house churches to help pioneer the creation of affinity conferences. The creation of ten nongeographical affinity conferences with an initial constituency of three hundred house churches each could be achieved by 2012. At that time, perhaps earlier, each of those 6,500 existing small churches would be offered an array of choices including (a) continuing their historic affiliation with a geographically defined conference, (b) continuing their affiliation with an affinity conference they joined a few years earlier, (c) requesting affiliation with one of these house church conferences, or (d) helping to pioneer a new affinity conference.

Would those be more attractive options to members of those small United Methodist congregations than the alternatives they often hear of, (a) merge with another church or (b) disband?

Why would a denomination that places a high value on every congregation owning and maintaining a separate meeting place and on seminary-trained ministerial leadership even consider the possibility of encouraging the proliferation of these small lay-led worshiping communities?

The obvious number-one motivation, of course, is this would be one component of a larger strategy to fulfill the Great Commission. Tens of thousands of churchgoing Protestant Christians clearly prefer the intimacy, the mutual support, the spontaneity, the informality, the fellowship, the caring, and the institutional simplicity of the small worshiping community. This would be a channel to reach and relate to that slice of the population.

Second, this wheel already has been invented. One version is described in the New Testament. A rapidly growing model is in the Third World. The "made in America" model exists and is waiting to be studied and adapted.

Third, all of the research on both the dynamics of human associations and the actual size of congregations in American Protestantism supports the contention that seven-to-thirty-five is the "natural" size of a worshiping community.

Fourth, the four options described earlier enlarge the list of action plans available to existing small churches.

Fifth, the lay-led house church model is the logical choice for those who object to the high cost of owning and maintaining real estate and/or the escalating costs of compensation for ordained ministers.

Sixth, those who are ideologically committed to expanding the ministry of the laity will discover this often is one of the primary motivations behind the creation of these nontraditional independent worshiping communities.

Seventh, from an empire-building perspective, the creation of this type of affinity judicatory adds another entry point for future members. Where does the house church member go who is now seeking more than what that intimate fellowship can offer? One alternative is to join a large nondenominational church. A second alternative could be to go to a larger congregation affiliated with the same denomination with which that house church is affiliated.

Eighth, what is the next step on the journey of that nondenominational house church that has attracted too many worshipers to continue as a small house church? To unilaterally invent its own future? To switch its allegiance to a nongeographical affinity judicatory consisting of ex-house churches that earlier outgrew that model and to learn from the experiences of others?

Ninth, all affinity judicatories should be organized to challenge and enable congregational leaders to benefit from the wisdom gained by others. One big gap in that network of affinity judicatories is the one created by and for house churches. Which denomination will be the first to act to fill that vacuum? Or should that responsibility be left to someone else?

Finally, we come back to the question of what is the future of your denomination? From this observer's perspective the darkest future lies ahead of those denominations committed to either (a) continued intradenominational quarreling and/or (b) keeping dying institutions and traditions alive for a few more decades. The brightest future lies ahead for those denominations that concentrate their resources and creativity on giving births to new ways to fulfill the Great Commission.

Creating affinity judicatories for house churches could be the least threatening and the most productive venture for those denominational leaders who are prepared to create new models of the American Protestant church for the twenty-first century.

What's the Point?

In addition to demonstrating the continuing attractiveness of the number forty-four, this long list of examples of affinity networks and judicatories is offered here for several reasons.

First, while far from exhaustive, it illustrates the range of possibilities.

Second, the list also illustrates that the old system of using two or three categories for describing congregations is obsolete. In the 1950s, for example, a widely used system consisted of three categories—rural, urban, and suburban. Earlier systems were based on the language used for worship. In classifying congregations, the United States Census of Religious Bodies of 1906 used fourteen sets of categories, (a) denomination, (b) language, (c) race, (d) year organized, (e) population of the host city or outside of large cities, (f) value of church property, (g) debt on property, (h) church-owned parsonage, (i) Sunday school, (j) membership, (k) seating capacity of worship center, (l) gender of members, (m) financial expenditures, and (n) ministerial salaries.

Most of the forty-four examples of potential affinity judicatories described here fit into one of six categories, (a) primary constituency, (b) size, (c) point of intervention in the lives of people (life cycle, faith journey, ethnicity, or marital status), (d) community setting, (e) staffing, or (f) specialized role.

What system does your denomination use in placing congregations in appropriate categories? Is it location of the meeting place? Race? Language? Baptisms? Number of dollars sent to denominational headquarters? Amount of financial subsidy received by that congregation? Size of ministerial staff? Growth curve? Date organized? Credentials of the clergy?

Which system is most useful in resourcing congregations to fulfill the Great Commission?

Third, this list also illustrates the larger trend toward specialization in the American economy. Restaurants, high schools, hospitals, grocery stores, farms, colleges and universities, magazines, pharmacies, radio stations, motor vehicle manufacturers, motion picture theaters, commercial airlines, brokerage houses, discount stores, retirement centers, home builders, employers, cities, private elementary schools, financial institutions, and disaster relief organizations are among the contemporary examples of differentiation. Each one attempts to communicate to potential future constituents a distinctive identity that distinguishes it from its competitors. Nearly all Protestant megachurches also seek to project a distinctive identity.

The specialists are replacing the generalists all across the American landscape! Should your denominational system be organized on the assumption that every affiliated congregation has the resources to fulfill the expectations and meet all the personal and spiritual needs of everyone? Do you believe one size can fit all and therefore a geographically defined regional judicatory can resource all sizes, types, and specialized roles of congregations?

Or do you believe the time has arrived for your denomination to take the initiative in creating affinity networks and affinity judicatories? Or do you believe you can depend on paradenominational organizations, entrepreneurial individuals, and other organizations to fill that vacuum?

Finally, and most important, this list is included here to illustrate a central theme of this book. The best single source of wisdom and insights for congregational leaders designing a ministry plan for their church for the twenty-first century is to go and learn from the experiences of others in similar circumstances. The closer that matches, the more likely that will be a relevant and productive learning experience.

Do You Believe in the Learning Curve?

One of the most important benefits of affinity judicatories could be in the process of ministerial placement. Four trends on the ecclesiastical scene have transformed the context for ministerial placement. Thanks to such technological achievements as the telephone, low cost commercial air travel, television, audiotapes, e-mail, Web sites, and videotapes, what formerly were regional, and largely intradenominational ministerial marketplaces are being replaced by national ministerial marketplaces that often cross denominational boundaries. The Southern Baptist minister in Kentucky moves to revitalize a United Methodist church in Texas. The Lutheran pastor in Maryland accepts a call to a nondenominational church in Illinois. The United Church of Christ minister moves to serve an independent church in Arizona. The Conservative Baptist minister in Colorado accepts a call to a Baptist General Conference church in Minnesota.

The second trend is the recent slow and gradual shrinkage in the number of denominational officials who act on the conviction that God has called them to be gatekeepers. The tradition-driven gatekeepers believed they had a responsibility to restrict the list of potential candidates for any vacant pulpit. That role flourished in those religious traditions organized around distrust of congregational leadership, but it is being undermined by the emergence of the national ministerial marketplace, by the demand for good matches, and by the erosion of trust by the laity in denominational leadership.

The third trend is a product of the increasing competition among Christian congregations in America to reach, attract, serve, welcome, and assimilate new generations of future church-goers. As the influence of brand names or denominational labels decreases among church shoppers seeking a new church home, the value of a "good match" increases in importance. In the ideal world the gifts, skills, personality, theological position, age, potential tenure, experience, priorities in ministry, and philosophy of ministry of the next pastor will closely match the needs of that congregation as it lives out the next chapter of its history. The higher the quality of that match, the higher the probability of a fruitful next chapter. A simple example is when the senior minister at the large downtown church retires after thirty years, that congregation does not call the thirty-five-year-old founding pastor of a new suburban mission now averaging seven hundred at worship. Instead it calls the forty-year-old pastor of another very large downtown church.

That introduces the fourth component of the contemporary institutional context. This is called the learning curve. During the past quarter century, a growing number of scholars have been researching this subject. Why is that elementary school teacher more competent and far more confident in classroom control in her fourth year as a third-grade teacher than she was in the fall of her first year? Why is this surgical team more proficient than that one in minimally invasive cardiac surgery? Why is the accident rate among sixteen-year-old female drivers so much higher than among nineteen-year-old female drivers? Why does the new president of the United States or the newly elected governor include at least two or three persons from the campaign trail among that leader's inner circle in that new office?

The call to be an effective parish pastor is a far more challenging and difficult assignment today than it was in 1955 or 1985! The learning curve is both steeper and longer. Equally important, the learning curve for the loving shepherd of a relatively stable congregation averaging 125 at worship in rural Iowa has very little overlap with the learning curve for the team leader planting a new mission in suburban Des Moines. The learning curve for the recently arrived second pastor of an Afro-centric congregation in Chicago founded in 1970 will differ greatly from the learning curve ahead of the recently arrived fifth pastor of a black church in Chicago also founded in 1970.

Critics of the learning curve argue that everyone needs a new challenge as part of being a lifelong learner. Thus the pastor who has served three pastorates with rural Anglo churches in central Florida for the past two decades will benefit from the challenge of serving a Cuban-American church in Miami.

To this observer that parallels the argument that the forty-seven-year-old neurologist who has spent the last two decades as a highly successful brain surgeon could spend the next two decades as a surgeon in urology. That could be a challenging second career for the surgeon, but I do not want to be his first patient when he makes that switch to urology!

The parallel question for officials responsible for ministerial placement is who is your number-one client? The pastor who wants to move? Or the congregation seeking a new pastor?

When ministers in the traditional geographically defined regional judicatory change pastorates within that judicatory, there is a high probability that also means a significant change in the culture, role, size, priorities, values, personality, local traditions, and community setting. That often means that pastor moves from a relatively high point on the learning curve appropriate for that congregation to a much lower spot on the learning curve that is appropriate for that next pastorate.

A simple and not uncommon example of the differences in learning curves is illustrated by three congregations seeking a new pastor. All three are affiliated with the same regional judicatory. One vacancy is a church in a county seat town with a population of 2,800. That congregation was organized in 1888 and is the only church of that denomination in the county. For the past forty years worship attendance has averaged between 120 and 140.

The second vacancy is in a congregation in the city housing the state capitol. It was founded by First Church downtown in 1922 as a new mission to serve a newly developed residential neighborhood. It peaked in average worship attendance at 263 in 1952. Last year worship attendance averaged eighty-five. That congregation owns eleven off-street parking spaces.

The third vacancy is a congregation founded in 1988. The founding pastor, now age forty-two, resigned last month to take a position in the national headquarters of that denomination. Last year the two nontraditional Sunday morning worship services attracted a combined average attendance of 438 at that three-acre site. Most of those worshipers were born after 1960. For the past year this congregation has been discussing the option of a complete relocation of the meeting place to a much larger site versus becoming a two-site church.

The learning curves before the next pastor in those three congregations display minimal overlap!

If those three congregations were affiliated with three different affinity judicatories, the search for a new pastor might be both easier and also more likely to produce a good match.

The first of those three congregations might be affiliated with an affinity judicatory consisting of similar size congregations in similar community settings. The second could be part of an affinity judicatory consisting of ex-neighborhood churches.

That third congregation could be affiliated with an affinity judicatory consisting of numerically growing new missions founded in the 1980s. Three or four dozen have been forced to relocate to a larger site. A dozen or more have chosen the two-site option. Thus that affinity judicatory not only could offer a productive learning environment for leaders torn between those two options, it also could be a happy hunting ground in that search for a new pastor.

What do these have in common? Trading an old car in for a new motor vehicle? Retiring from the labor force? Enrolling in graduate school? Having a tooth extracted? Committing murder? Writing a book? Searching for a new pastor? Advancing up the learning curve? Giving birth to a baby? It's easier the second time.

It also is easier to find a good match in the next pastor if that congregation is affiliated with an affinity judicatory!

Is This a Dumb Idea?

After floating several trial balloons, it appears most of the arguments against this suggested paradigm shift are reflected in these seven comments.

1. "It threatens the status quo and therefore will never be adopted!"

2. "It is good for the people in our churches to associate with and to learn from different ministries and people in churches that are unlike their own. We need to affirm diversity and hetereogeneity rather than encourage homogeneity. Too many of our parishioners now live and work in socially isolated pockets of homogeneity."

3. "Our geographically defined regional judicatory, together with the resources available from our national denominational agencies, can respond effectively for pleas for help from any and all of our congregations. Don't try to fix what ain't broke!"

4. "This is a great idea! It would be even better, however, if

there were nondenominational affinity networks, not judicatories. Creating these as nondenominational or interdenominational affinity networks could be a big step down the path to greater Christian unity. While that probably will erode the loyalty of those congregations to their denomination, we accept that as one of the price tags on ecumenism."

5. "Uniformity has been and continues to be one of the central goals of our denomination, and this would destroy uniformity."

6. "A primary role for our midlevel judicatories is to collect money from congregations and send at least one-third of those dollars to fund our national church. This could destroy the financial foundation of our denomination."

7. "The only way this could be implemented would be if two or three denominations with different polities agreed to merge and the affinity-based judicatory would be a part of the larger compromise required to create a new organizational structure for what would be a new denomination."

A more productive response could be to examine alternative strategies, but that requires another chapter.

CHAPTER TEN

TWELVE ALTERNATIVE SCENARIOS

I s the paradigm shift from a geographical to an affinity princi-ple the only approach to reversing the numerical decline of the large mainline denominations in American Protestant-ism?

NO!

Is it the strategy most likely to result in a fast and substantial reversal of that membership curve?

NO!

Why recommend it? Three reasons. First, it builds on what already is happening. It does not require radical or untested changes. Second, it has a high probability of success. It builds on the existing assets of the creativity, initiative, and skills of con-gregational leaders. It is based on the conviction that when Christians are challenged to do ministry, rather than send money to hire someone else to do ministry on their behalf, the ceiling is raised on what can happen. Third, the record of nondenomina-tional affinity networks over the past few decades suggests a high probability of success for this model of denominational systems.

Do you prefer a strategy with a higher probability of success? If so, another alternative can be found in the history books.

Focus on Church Planting

When did the Congregational Church experience a relatively high rate of numerical growth? During the 1880–1906 era. That was when 2,677 of the 5,713 Congregational churches in exis-tence in 1906 were established. (See Appendix F for more details.)

When did the Presbyterian Church in the United States of America experience an era of rapid numerical growth? During those same twenty-seven years a total of more than 3,312 of the 7,935 congregations in existence in 1906 were founded.

When did the Presbyterian Church in the United States (the southern antecedent of what is the Presbyterian Church [U.S.A.] of today) experience rapid growth? During that same 1880–1906 era when 1,314 of the 3,114 congregations in existence in 1906 were established.

During those same twenty-seven years, 2,974 of the 6,845 Episcopal parishes in existence in 1906 were organized. The two dozen Lutheran denominations in existence in 1906 reported a combined total of 12,703 parishes. Of the 11,930 reporting a date of organization, 7,318 or 61 percent named a year in that 1880–1906 time period. In 1906 7,937 of the 8,272 Northern Baptist congregations reported their date of organization and 3,333 identified a year in that 1880–1906 period. The Christian Church (Disciples of Christ) included 8,294 congregations in 1906. A total of 5,678 reported their date of organization and a majority of those reporting, 3,742, reported their origins traced back to that 1880–1906 era.

The six predecessor denominations of today's United Methodist Church reported a combined total of 57,087 congregations in 1906. Of the 42,441 reporting their date of establishment, nearly one-half or 20,083 named a year in that 1880–1906 post–Civil War era.

During those twenty-seven years the population of the United States increased by approximately thirty-five million. A century later, during the twenty-seven years from 1975 through 2001, the population of the United States increased by seventy million.

In other words, the denominational systems described here gave a high priority to new church development in an era when the annual net increase in the American population averaged 1.3 million. In recent years, when the population growth has averaged 2.6 million annually, church planting has received a much lower priority by these same Protestant traditions.

One response to that pattern is, "Back in 1890 the United States was seriously underchurched. Today this country is overchurched."

That statement does not agree with the historical record. The United States Bureau of the Census reported the nation's population was seventy million in 1890, and they counted 165,177 religious congregations of all faiths. That averages out to one religious congregation for every 424 residents in 1890.

By 1906 that ratio had dropped to one religious congregation for every 410 residents. At the end of 2001 that ratio was estimated to be one religious congregation, including house churches and non-Christian religions for every 760 residents.

Do we know that implementing a strategy to plant more new missions during the last two-thirds of the twentieth century by these predominantly Anglo mainline denominations would have reversed the numerical decline they have experienced?

Of course not! What the historical record does reveal, however, is that those religious bodies that have increased the number of affiliated congregations also have experienced a substantial increase in the number of constituents. During the twentieth century the Southern Baptist Convention nearly doubled the number of congregations and increased their membership eightfold. The Church of Jesus Christ of Latter-day Saints increased the number of congregations from slightly more than 600 in 1900 to well over 11,000 in 2000. That coincided with an increase from 200,000 to nearly 5 million members. The Seventh-day Adventist Church reported 1,772 congregations and 66,000 members in 1906. At the end of 2000 those numbers had grown to 4,500 congregations with nearly 900,000 American members. The Christian Reformed Church in North America reported 28,000 members in 166 congregations in 1906 and nearly 140,000 members in 735 churches in 2000. The Baptist General Conference, another of several success stories of the Americanization of an immigrant church, reported nearly 100,000 members in 591 congregations in 1968. By the end of 2001 those numbers had grown to nearly 145,000 members in 900 congregations. That 50 percent increase in the number of congregations had been accompanied by a 50 percent increase in membership and more than a 50 percent increase in worship attendance.

Another example is the Assemblies of God, which was not founded until 1914, and by the end of the twentieth century included 1.5 million members in 12,084 American congregations.

A different explanation declares that the key is NOT new church development. This perspective contends the crucial variable is the high priority given to evangelism. An increase in the number of congregations and the number of constituents are both a product of that emphasis on evangelism.

Why Not?

A persuasive case can be made that the closest to a guaranteed strategy to reverse the numerical decline of the mainline denominations in American Protestantism would be to devote 85 to 95 percent of all available denominational resources to planting new missions. That would mean defining new church development as the core purpose of both regional and national denominational agencies. Who would resource the existing congregations? Who would provide the prophetic voice on social justice issues? Who would raise the money to finance church-related institutions such as colleges, homes, camps, seminaries, and other agencies?

How many new missions should be planted each year if that is the heart of the strategy?

One guideline if new church development is to be the core purpose of a denominational system calls for launching a number that is the equivalent of 1 percent of all existing affiliated congregations every year to remain on a plateau in size. A second calls for new missions to be equal to 2 percent of all existing congregations if the goal is numerical growth. The third plateau applies when the goal includes both numerical growth and transforming a predominantly Anglo denomination into a multicultural body. That raises the bar to 3 percent annually.

That 1 percent goal translates into 350 new missions annually for The United Methodist Church and approximately one hundred each for the Evangelical Lutheran Church in America, the Presbyterian Church (U.S.A.), and the Assemblies of God. A similar goal would be seventy-five new missions annually for the Episcopal Church, sixty each for the United Church of Christ and the American Baptist Churches in the U.S.A., and forty annually for the Christian Church (Disciples of Christ). Double those numbers if the goal is to produce significant numerical growth, and triple them if the goal is to become a multicultural religious body.

A goal of two hundred new missions annually probably should include at least seventy-five that are designed to be very large congregations averaging a least eight hundred at worship by the end of five years. A different design would be used for another seventy-five planned to be midsized congregations leveling off with an average worship attendance in the 350-to-500 bracket. The other fifty might be planned to fill a precisely defined niche. That could include serving couples in intercultural marriages or residents of retirement communities or home schoolers or never-married adults or graduate students in a large research university or any one of a hundred other affinity groups.

If this strategy carries with it such a high probability of success, why not recommend it?

1. With the exception of the Assemblies of God, it is unlikely that the current policymaking processes used in the large and predominantly Anglo Protestant denominations would allow such a large proportion of available resources to be designated for new church development. Why recommend a strategy that is politically unlikely to be acceptable?

2. Few of these denominations have the infrastructure, the staff, the political support, and the institutional culture required to implement this strategy. While it would be relatively easy, through designated second-mile giving by individuals, to raise the required funds, it would be far more difficult to mobilize the necessary managerial capability. It is far easier to launch new congregations that plateau with an average worship attendance under a hundred or close before their tenth birthday.

3. Most important, the emergence of literally thousands of very large and highly attractive Protestant churches in the United States since 1960 has sharply increased the competition for future constituents. A hundred years ago the new church that was averaging a hundred people at worship by its fifth birthday was not only economically viable, it also was widely considered to be a success story. A modest building on a half-acre site provided an attractive meeting place at a modest cost. A relatively large number of ministers were able to lead a new mission in achieving that goal in 1900. Today the demand is for a team of three full-time people plus a couple of part-time program specialists who can launch a new mission that will be averaging 450 to 600 at worship by the end of that crucial first year. Ten years later that new congregation will be meeting in a $5 million building on a twenty-to-two hundred-acre site. The demand for these teams greatly exceeds the supply!

The expectations of churchgoers in the United States born after 1960 are far more demanding than the expectations of the churchgoers born after 1860. That means using a large-church model in planting new missions.

4. While this new trend has received relatively limited attention, it is possible that the old focus on planting new missions is an obsolete concept. Why? First, the dollar cost to the sponsoring body is high and keeps going up. Second, and more important, the failure rate is high. Fewer than one-half of the new missions planted by the mainline Protestant denominations in the 1980s were (a) still in existence in 2000 and (b) averaging more than 150 at worship. Third, a disproportionately large number of the success stories tend to be found among the new missions sponsored by a congregation averaging more than two thousand at worship that are able to "export" the culture and skills for "how to do big church effectively."

In other words, the contemporary American ecclesiastical environment suggests a more productive strategy would place a high priority on encouraging the emergence of more very large congregations averaging between eight hundred and fifteen thousand at worship at one site rather than increasing the number averaging under three hundred at worship. A second priority could be to encourage the creation of more multisite congregations. A third priority could be to encourage congregations meeting in a functionally obsolete building on an inadequate site at what had become a poor location to make a fresh start and begin to write a new volume in their history in new facilities on a larger site at a better location. The fourth priority could be to challenge very large churches to export skill in how to "do large church effectively" by sponsoring new missions. The fifth priority could be denominationally sponsored new missions.

5. The successor to the old pattern of denominationally sponsored new missions appears to be the large-to-very-large church that, instead of sponsoring new missions, becomes a multisite church.

Invent and Play a New Game

The Forty Year Rule states that by the time they reach their fortieth birthday, institutions in the American economy tend to be driven by the past, by local traditions, by taking better care of the employees, by the real estate, by last year's budget, and by internal bureaucratic constraints. That generalization applies to automobile companies, public high schools, Protestant churches meeting at the same address for four decades or longer, magazines, college dormitories, grocery stores, hospitals, financial institutions, and scores of other institutions. One consequence is the majority do not make it to their fortieth birthday. A second is those that do usually choose one of five roads to the future, (a) continued decline, (b) merger, (c) dissolution, (d) an internal housecleaning of the executive staff, or (e) reinventing themselves for a new tomorrow.

One new game calls for the denomination to reinvent itself as an adopting parent. An attractive alternative emerges if the process for designing a denominational strategy for the twenty-first century is driven by these four forces, (a) a desire for institutional survival, (b) a goal of increased demographic diversity among the constituents, (c) a goal to increase the degree of theological pluralism within that religious tradition, and (d) the need for a redistribution of wealth and income.

Instead of attempting to recreate the 1870–1960 emphasis on *planting* new missions, the focus is on *adopting* relatively new non-denominational churches and those congregations related to a denomination that affirm dual affiliation. Numerically growing independent churches that need to expand their physical facilities will be invited to become members of that adopting denominational regional judicatory.

Why would a five-year-old independent Latino congregation or a four-year-old independent Chinese church or a seven-year-old independent African American or Korean American church want to affiliate with your denomination? A past quarter century provides scores of answers to that question. The adopting denomination is prepared to offer a generous financial grant and/or a below-market interest rate loan to enable that independent church to enlarge its physical facilities and/or to expand its ministry. An attractive package could consist of (a) free advice on designing a ministry plan, (b) an outright grant of $200,000, and

(c) a low interest loan of $300,000. Thus for $1 million every year in grants and $1.5 million in loans from a revolving fund in the denominational foundation, a regional judicatory could adopt an average of five new congregations annually and also increase the demographic diversity within the constituency.

The price tags on this strategy include (a) an affirmation of unrestricted congregational autonomy, (b) a full recognition of the ordination and ministerial standing of pastors who never attended seminary, (c) the capability and willingness to raise the required capital funds, and (d) zero requirements for each member congregation to support the denominational position on social, economic, political, doctrinal, and polity issues.

This would be an attractive option for those religious traditions willing to accept this role as an "adopting church" and also able to fulfill the responsibilities that go with that role. For at least a couple of mainline American Protestant traditions, the big barrier could be approving the concept that one congregation can be affiliated concurrently with two or more denominations.

One explanation for the numerical shrinkage of those seven large and predominantly Anglo mainline American Protestant denominations is they are too large, too tradition-driven, too pluralistic in terms of values and goals, and too politicized in their decision-making processes to be able to agree on and adopt a strategy for renewal.

The obvious response to that expression of institutional paralysis is for the discontented to leave and create a new congregation or even a new denomination. That exodus of the discontented leaving to help create the new represents a major strand in American church history, especially since 1950.

A more mature expression of that course of action also calls for inventing and playing a new game. This new game begins by recognizing that the differences within each of these seven large mainline Protestant denominations are greater than the differences among them. The next step would be to peacefully divide into several new and highly homogeneous denominations. In most, if not all, of these seven denominations, dependency path theory would dictate that the majority of congregations would vote to continue with the "mother church." That would limit the new "splinter" denominations to perhaps two dozen, each with three hundred to six thousand affiliated congregations. Would a new denomination with only one thousand affiliated congregations be viable? That depends on the definition of purpose, but with a thousand congregations it would be larger than eight out of ten religious bodies in American Christianity today.

Why not pursue this strategy?

1. It probably could not reach the agenda of any of these seven denominations.

2. If it did, the process of arriving at an equitable division of assets and liabilities might dominate the agenda for several years.

3. It is much easier for discontented church members to depart quietly. It also is easier to watch as the majority of congregations report an aging and numerically shrinking constituency than it is to open the door for the departure of discontented congregations. This means replacing the old game of perpetuating dying empires with a new game called kingdom building.

The Problem Is Our People

The third, and for many the most attractive of these four strategies calls for concentrating resources on raising the level of quality in all the existing affiliated congregations. Focus on renewing and revitalizing the existing congregations.

Why is that not placed first, rather than third on this list of alternative strategies? One reason is because it is much easier to create the new than to renew the old. It is easier to give birth to the new than to transform the old.

Second, and more important, this third alternative tempts people to play the blame game. The heart of the problem is the incompetence of our pastors. Should we blame them? Or blame the theological schools they attended? Or is the real problem our theologically and biblically illiterate laity? Our problems are rooted in the people, not in the system.

Since we cannot dismiss them, let us design continuing educa-tion events for both our most incompetent pastors and our least effective volunteer leaders. Thus the blame game naturally tends to lead to an effort to create strength and nurture creativity by focusing on weakness.

The paradigm shift recommended in this book is based on two different assumptions. The first is many of the problems are rooted in the system, not in the personnel. The second is to iden-tify strengths and build on assets.

Design and Implement a Church Growth Strategy

For those who prefer to minimize disruptions to the present denominational systems and who also enjoy an abundance of cre-ative and venturesome leadership, an easier course of action could be to design and implement a strategy for numerical growth resembling this ten-point plan. The easiest components to imple-ment are listed first and subsequent ones are increasingly difficult.

1. Adopt independent or nondenominational congregations seeking a denominational affiliation. Most of these probably will be either relatively new immigrant churches or ethnic minority churches.

This is an especially attractive strategy for those denomina-tions that have a revolving fund of *denominationally owned assets* that were created to make construction loans to congregations. This could be a high-risk venture, however, if the model is a sav-ings-and-loan association that guarantees depositors a 6 percent annual return on short-term deposits and makes twenty year loans at 7 percent. If and when interest rates go up and the depos-itors demand either the return of their deposits or a much higher interest rate, this can turn into a financial and legal disaster!

2. Encourage very large and numerically growing congrega-tions to export their skill in "how to do big church in the twenty-first century" by becoming multisite congregations.

3. Assemble teams of three-to-five gifted individuals, each of whom is driven by a passion for evangelism, to create what will be a large church from week one and averaging at least five hundred at worship by the end of the first year.

4. Turn to very large and numerically growing teaching churches for the next generation of parish pastors, senior ministers, and program specialists (both lay and ordained). Focus on those who have enjoyed at least five years of happy, effective, and productive ministry as heavily involved volunteers and/or as paid staff. In screening second- or third-career candidates, focus on those who have achieved success in school, in the secular labor force, in marriage, and in one or more hobbies. (Three out of four is acceptable. Two out of four is unacceptable.)

5. Encourage and enable many of your existing congregations to move up out of the service business into the experience economy and eventually into the transformation business. (Read B. Joseph Pine II and James H. Gilmore, *The Experience Economy* [Boston: Harvard Business School Press, 1999].)

6. Solicit proposals from interested parties to plant new missions. Each proposal must cover every component of the design from the constituency to be reached to the resources required for implementation. Fund those that combine an excellent plan with a competent leadership team.

This covers those components of a larger strategy that have the highest success rate.

7. Encourage those congregations with the necessary resources to open and operate a Christian day school for ages three through nine or older, adding one grade every year. This would be one component of a much larger package of ministries with families that include young children, not simply a community service project.

8. Encourage numerically growing congregations meeting in an obsolete building on an inadequate site at a second or third-rate location to relocate and write a new chapter in their history in new facilities on a larger site at a better location.

9. Help interested congregations design and implement a program to improve their capability to assimilate newcomers.

10. Seek to build agreement that the "normal" tenure for a parish pastor is between twenty-five and forty years.

Those interested in a more comprehensive thirty-five-point strategy may want to add the following. The number indicates their place on this longer list that ranges from the highest success rate at the top to the lowest success rate at the end.

31. Send individual pastors out on a three-year assignment to plant new missions with volunteers who prefer to be members of a small church. Build the new mission around a network of one-to-one interpersonal relationships with the pastor at the hub of that network. Every three or four years replace the pastor.

34. Focus your resources on revitalizing small and numerically shrinking congregations with an aging constituency.

35. Merge two small, weak, and numerically shrinking churches. Sell one meeting place and use the better of the two as the meeting place for the merged church. The goal is to create strength by combining weakness. (The reason this is number 35 is it does not belong in a church growth strategy. This option should be number 3 on a larger strategy to reduce the number of affiliated congregations and/or to reduce the membership.)

It should be emphasized this is a denominationally driven numerical growth strategy. That is NOT the same as a strategy for helping every congregation to make fulfilling the Great Commission its central organizing principle! It also does not resemble a design to encourage congregational leaders to learn from their peers in similar settings.

Instead of recommending a paradigm shift that many will view as disruptive, why not recommend a multifaceted denominational growth strategy such as this one? Four reasons.

1. This alternative ignores the fact that congregations, not denominations, constitute the front line of mission in America today.

2. Comprehensive growth strategies have been around for four decades, but few denominations have been able to design and implement one with acceptable outcomes.

3. If the heart of the problem is systemic, adopting a church growth strategy without changing the system may produce more frustration than hope.

4. Experience suggests when the system is transformed, positive results do follow. One example is the Southern Baptist Convention of South Carolina.[1] A second is the Diocese of Texas of the Episcopal Church where the system was reinvented.[2] What happened? Between 1993 and 1997 the one hundred American dioceses in the Episcopal Church collectively reported an increase of nearly twenty thousand in average worship attendance. The second greatest increase was in the Diocese of Atlanta where average worship attendance increased from 15,532 in 1993 to 17,405 in 1997, an increase of 1,873, followed by the Diocese of Central Florida with an increase of 1,481 or 16.4 percent. In the Diocese of Texas average worship attendance increased by 4,205 in four years.[3] It must be added that forty-three dioceses reported a decrease in worship attendance over that four-year period.

Eight Other Alternatives

From this observer's perspective and value system, the most desirable strategy for the larger mainline Protestant denominations in America calls for redesigning the current systems on the assumption congregations do represent the front line of mission in contemporary America. Reinventing the definition and role of the midlevel denominational judicatories could be a relatively easy, fast, and effective way to accomplish that. Far more difficult to adopt and implement would be the four strategies described in the earlier pages of this chapter—plant many more new missions, divide the very large and heterogeneous denominations into smaller and more homogeneous bodies, raise the level of performance in existing congregations or design and implement a comprehensive church growth strategy.

That short list, however, does not even begin to exhaust the list of alternative strategies. This point can be illustrated by a brief discussion of eight other options.

1. The most tempting is to declare that the present system is effective and should be continued. Ignore the shrinking numbers. Ignore demands for an annual performance review. Ignore that growing number of congregations going to "outside" vendors for the resources they need. Ignore the impact of continued intra-denominational quarreling. Celebrate the fact the glass still is nearly half full. Focus on the victories wherever they can be found and ignore the more disturbing long-term trends.

2. Staff the geographically defined regional judicatories with volunteers from congregations. They may be able to make helping congregations to fulfill the Great Commission the number-one priority for that denomination.

3. Dissolve all existing regional midlevel judicatories and deploy national staff to work with congregationally created affinity networks.

4. The lowest cost option would be to close out the existing denominational systems, except for pension boards and foundations, and encourage denominationally affiliated congregations to follow the tens of thousands of nondenominational Protestant congregations that currently are relying on vendors in the ecclesiastical marketplace for resources. That is a highly competitive and creative free market with the capability for rapid expansion. It also is exceptionally sensitive to the needs of congregational leaders.

5. Delegate the responsibility for fulfilling the Great Commission to those congregations and denominational bodies that believe that is a high priority and focus on going down the road to Christian unity. History suggests those are different roads, and a denomination can travel down one or the other, but not both concurrently.

One of the two big existing roads toward Christian unity has been in the planning stage for four decades and now has a new sign, "Churches Uniting in Christ." Nine denominations currently are working together to make that an attractive highway into the twenty-first century.

A second road toward Christian unity has been in the design stage for several years. The current list of engineers designing this road comes from the Episcopal Church, the Evangelical Lutheran Church in America, the Presbyterian Church (U.S.A.), the United Church of Christ, the Moravian Church in America, and the Reformed Church in America.

Both of these two roads are designed to attract Christians who prefer to focus on what one religious tradition has in common with other religious bodies. The driving assumption is all roads lead to the same heaven, so why not come together now and travel the same road with one another in this life?

A third, and the widest of these three roads into the twenty-first century has a big sign at the entrance with one word on it. That word is UNITY. It is DIFFERENTIATION. Each of the religious bodies choosing this road insists it has a distinctive and clearly defined belief system as well as a set of practices that differentiate it from other religious bodies in America. Each construction crew, instead of working together, builds its own lane in this wide road. Currently the most diligent construction crews come from the Roman Catholic Church, the Church of Jesus Christ of Latter-day Saints, the Church of God in Christ, the Assemblies of God, the Southern Baptist Convention, the Lutheran Church-Missouri Synod, a couple of thousand nondenominational Protestant megachurches, and at least five hundred other relatively small religious traditions in America.

If you count the number of churchgoers, it is easy to understand why this third road has to be three or four times the combined width of those first two roads.

6. For many American Protestant Christians, the challenge to renew the old mainline denominations evokes laughter, a big yawn, a shrug, or a declaration, "I don't have a dog in that fight." They leave to worship with a nondenominational congregation or with a denominationally affiliated church organized around fulfilling the Great Commission.

A smaller group, however, are strong believers in the merits of denominational systems. They rally fellow believers with the same ideological convictions. Their operational slogan is, "Don't waste your time and energy trying to renew the old, come with us and together we will pioneer the creation of a new denomination. During the last half of the twentieth century this turned out to be an attractive alternative to Congregationalists, Lutherans, Presbyterians. Episcopalians, and others. Therefore it must be on this list of options for the twenty-first century. Schism is not an obsolete concept on the American ecclesiastical scene!

7. A more peaceful response to the call for the right of self-determination was pioneered by major league baseball, football, and basketball. After a designated period of time, a player can either sign a new contract with his former team or become a free agent. Free agency conveys the right not only to switch teams, but also to change conferences or leagues.

This is NOT a new idea! American military organizations have used the concept of term contracts for service by individuals for generations.

The equivalent on the ecclesiastical scene would be a declaration by several cooperative religious bodies shortly after Easter. "A year from this coming July, every congregation will become a free agent. Each congregation will be asked to choose its denominational affiliation for the next five years. Each congregation will be free to re-enlist in the same denomination, switch midlevel judicatories within the same denomination, or to enlist with a different religious tradition. The laity and the clergy have enjoyed this right of free agency for decades, we are now extending it to congregations. Pray for God's guidance as you determine the future for your congregation."

8. Perhaps the most attractive alternative would be to copy success. The ecclesiastical landscape is attracting a growing number of vendors who rely on the fees-for-services system for financing their ministry. Publishing houses are among the veterans in this approach to resourcing congregations. The value of it is a strong incentive to be sensitive to the needs of congregations and individuals.

Every midlevel regional judicatory could switch to the fees-for-services system for funding within a space of two-to-three years. This could be the easiest alternative to implement in this book— but it does requires a venturesome spirit.

What is the future of your denomination? The central paradigm shift of creating affinity judicatories described in this book is only one of many alternatives open to you. The dozen other options described in this chapter are offered to demonstrate that really is a long list. Add to the list. Compare one option with all the others. Which one comes closest to matching what you believe God is calling your denomination to be and to be doing in the decades ahead?

A THIRD PARADIGM
SHIFT

T his book advocates three paradigm shifts. The big and
highly visible one is to supplement, and perhaps eventually replace, the traditional geographically defined
regional judicatories with affinity networks and affinity judicatories.

The second calls for an expansion in the number and variety
of learning experiences for both lay volunteers and paid congregational staff. (See chapter 3.)

The third paradigm shift is far more subjective and less obvious. This calls for a new approach to defining the identity of
these denominationally affiliated congregations. Historically
denominational affiliation has been the core component of the
identity and public image of these churches. The denominational
affiliation usually is represented in the name, in the location in

the Yellow Pages of the telephone book, on the sign out front, in the doctrinal position, in the ministerial standing of the pastor, in the weekly ad in the local newspaper, in the rulebook used in governance, in determining the destination of most benevolence dollars, in the choice of a hymnal, in the selection of educational resources, in the standards used for determining membership, and in the criteria followed for inviting guest speakers as well as in the general public image.

This proposal does not call for discarding that denominational label. This plan is designed to enhance loyalty to that congregation's denominational system.

When Warren Buffett was asked to reflect on *Fortune* magazine's list of the ten most admired for-profit American corporations for 1998, he commented, "People are voting for the artist, not the painting." His point was several corporations were among the ten most admired because of their leadership. Jack Welch, Bill Gates, Michael Eisner, and Warren Buffett were the primary reason for General Electric, Microsoft, Disney, and Berkshire Hathaway being included among the top ten.[1]

A similar pattern can be seen in American Protestantism during the past century. The public image of scores of Protestant congregations was the artist, not the painting. The local or national image was and often is either the founding pastor or the current senior minister, not the denomination. Many of these nationally and world famous churches do not even carry a denominational label, or they carry it in the pocket rather than on their name tag.

That is the preferred option by many congregational leaders. Build our congregation around the gifts, personality, passion, priorities, communication skills, theological stance, vision, productive work habits, leadership style, and reputation of a long-tenured great preacher. This is the approach that wins the support of the laity who are convinced, "The future of our church depends on our getting the right minister." One flaw in that approach is most of these magnetic personalities are mortal and eventually leave that church to be with the Lord. An even more serious flaw is when that attractive personality leaves to be with someone else's spouse.

The paradigm shift suggested here is rather than build the identity of a congregation around the denominational affiliation, in an era when persons born after 1950 are far less likely to be motivated by institutional loyalties than were their parents or grandparents, build the identity of that congregation around what it is doing in ministry and how the lives of people are being transformed by those ministries. To return to the Pine-Gilmore book cited earlier, move from the brand name of an organization in the business of providing services (worship, education, fellowship, meals, care of children, religious rituals) to that fifth level of the transformation of people's lives.

Instead of defining the identity by the denominational label or the personality and gifts of the pastor or the real estate or the weekend schedule of services or local traditions, define that congregation's identity by its distinctive role in ministry.

What Do We Fix?

What should be done when a congregation is not fulfilling its potential in ministry? The old paradigm usually focused on one or more of three alternatives. One called for fixing the problem by replacing the pastor. A second called for more and better continuing education for that pastor. The third called for continuing education experiences or workshops for the volunteer lay leadership. Since the problem is in the people, the solution is to fix the people.

This new paradigm has two facets. One is to change the basis for defining the identity of a congregation from the denominational affiliation and/or the current pastor to defining each congregation's identity by its distinctive role in ministry. Instead of trying to fix the people, focus on fixing the system.

The first step in that process is for the congregational leaders to design a ministry plan that reflects what they believe God is calling that church to be and to be about in the years ahead. The second step in that process calls for those leaders to go and visit a contemporary working model of a church that matches their vision. They spend two to five days talking with, listening to, asking questions of, and studying what the leaders of that working model have done and are doing. They go back home and modify their tentative ministry plan by adapting what they have learned. A couple of months later, they visit another working model of their vision and repeat the process.

In the ideal world that first and second visit will be with leaders from a self-identified teaching church that displays two characteristics. First, the volunteers and paid staff have mastered the art of helping eager learners investigate what to them will be a "new way to do church" and to internalize those learnings.

Second, in the eyes of the visitors five or ten years ago that host congregation was close to a carbon copy of what "our church is today," but it now closely resembles the vision of what these visitors believe the Lord is calling their congregation to be a few years down the road. That match enables the teaching church to authentically model two scenarios. One, of course, is a working model of a relevant and effective church in the twenty-first century. The other is to model the path from "what we were" to "what we are now" and how the old was transformed into the new. A common example is the small neighborhood congregation founded in 1955 that has been transformed into the large regional church of today.

The leaders in those teaching churches benefit in several respects. They are forced to reflect carefully and thoughtfully on what they have done and why they did it that way. The occasional probing question stimulates them to consider possible improvements. They benefit from that ancient slogan, "The best way to learn a subject is to teach it." They learn church renewal as they teach it. Their level of self-esteem and self-confidence is raised when they realize visitors have come from great distances "to learn from what we're doing here." The volunteers in these teaching churches gain considerable personal satisfaction from these experiences. How do we reward hard working, deeply committed, and creative volunteers? One way is the sincere praise from outsiders who have come to learn from them.

CHAPTER TWELVE

TRADE-OFFS AND CONSEQUENCES

For at least three or four of the large mainline American Protestant denominations, the most serious tradeoff involved in adopting and implementing the strategy suggested in this book will be a radical change in the institutional culture of that religious tradition. This will be most apparent in those religious bodies that place a high value on institutional uniformity. By contrast, the higher the level of intradenominational agreement on a belief system, rather than on practices, the easier it will be to implement this strategy. The strategy recommended in this book is built on an affirmation of flexibility and customization in the practice of ministry, not on uniformity in practices.

One of the reasons behind the success of the welfare reform legislation signed into law in 1996 by President William J.

Clinton was that it granted a high degree of flexibility to the states. Likewise a Protestant strategy for heavily Catholic Massachusetts will not be the same as a Protestant strategy for heavily Catholic states such as Louisiana, New Mexico, and Wisconsin.

Uniformity or Customization?

Rather than adopting the organizational structure used by all other congregations in that particular religious tradition, this strategy calls for designing a customized ministry plan that is consistent with the purpose, role, type, size, and unique personality of congregations and is appropriate for the contemporary community setting in which that church is called to be engaged in ministry. Likewise this strategy is based on the assumption that the organizational structure of the denomination will be designed to help all congregations, even though they differ greatly from one another in culture, size, age, type, resources, community context, and leadership, concentrate on fulfilling the Great Commission. That calls for flexibility and variety, rather than uniformity, in that denominational structure.

This strategy is inconsistent with a "one approach fits all of the congregations in our tradition." One price tag on customization is the loss of uniformity. A current example is the increase in the number of denominationally affiliated congregations who rarely or never use their denominational hymnal.

Shepherds or Leaders?

Equally important is the style of ministerial leadership. This strategy is not appropriate for those religious traditions that operate on the assumption that any fully credentialed clergyperson can serve any congregation, regardless of type, size, history, role, community setting, or culture.

This strategy also is incompatible with a rules-driven religious culture that places a premium on parish pastors following "the party line." Implementation of this strategy requires an affirmation of entrepreneurial leaders who enjoy the challenge of pioneering a new tomorrow. It is NOT compatible with ministerial leaders who are comfortable waiting for "orders from headquarters" before planning for tomorrow. To use the frame of reference described by the late David Riesman in his book, *The Lonely Crowd*, published in 1950, this strategy will be most effective if implemented by leaders who are "inner-directed," rather than "tradition-directed." That raises two obvious questions. One is directed at the criteria denominations use to screen candidates for the ministry. The second concerns the expectations placed on theological seminaries as they socialize students preparing for the parish ministry.

One of the consequences of this emphasis on designing a customized ministry plan for every congregation and a greater reliance on entrepreneurial leadership is the necessity for relatively long pastorates. Those smaller and tradition-driven congregations that resemble one large social network with the pastor, who is a loving shepherd, at the hub of that network, usually can endure replacing one loving shepherd with another loving shepherd every few years. Many are comfortable sharing the time and affection of their loving shepherd with one or two other small churches if that can reduce their expenditures. For larger congregations, however, that have designed a twenty- or thirty-year ministry plan, a long pastorate usually is a crucial component for the implementation process.

Why talk about a twenty-to-thirty year time frame for planning? The obvious reason is that if it includes the construction or renovation of physical facilities, most governmental building codes include requirements that call for expensive permanent investments. It is more expensive to replace a five-year-old and now functionally obsolete worship center seating three hundred people than it is to replace a pastor.

A better reason for long pastorates is continuity in leadership. It is much easier to find a new loving shepherd to replace a departing loving shepherd than it is to find a new visionary leader with the same style, priorities, theological stance, skills, vision, energy, and goals as the departing visionary leader. It is even more difficult to find a new visionary leader who is both competent and comfortable in leading a congregation to implement a ministry plan adopted six years earlier with the leadership of a different visionary minister.

This is a minor issue for those denominations convinced the future lies with small Protestant congregations averaging fewer than 135 at worship, but it should be a top-of-the-agenda item for those denominations seriously interested in reaching American-born residents born after 1960.

A third consequence focuses on a question that is more subjective than either the issue of denominationwide uniformity or the leadership role and tenure of pastors.

What Is the Tie That Binds?

"What is the central organizing principle that describes your denominational culture? Do you believe it is a voluntary association of individual Christians and congregations who are bound together by a shared commitment? Or do you believe it more closely resembles the association that is based on a legal principle?[1] Citizens of the United States are members of a nation that is organized around formal rules describing rights, obligations, entitlements, duties, and relationships.

While Americans are bound together by a widely shared commitment to individual freedom, democracy, and self-determination, the United States of America is a nation organized on legal principles. It is not a voluntary association! Residents are required, for example, not simply encouraged, to pay taxes. Licenses are legal requirements for anyone seeking to engage in the practice of medicine or drive a motor vehicle or install the plumbing in an office building.

Those ten teenage boys who have gathered to play basketball on an outdoor court provided by the local park district constitute a voluntary association. All ten are volunteers. Each one retains the right to drop out and go home when he chooses to do so. While it is primarily a voluntary association, the ten have agreed on a few legal principles they call rules that do control the scoring and individual, as well as team, behavior. Those informal rules may even include a dress code for the players called "shirts and skins." The *primary* central organizing principle, however, is a shared commitment to play basketball on a warm Saturday afternoon.

In his eight "laws" describing the interrelationship of these two principles Lon L. Fuller points out that nearly every human association reflects both central organizing principles—shared commitment and legal obligations.[2]

By definition that is true for every denomination in American Protestantism. Those voluntary associations organized solely around shared commitment are associations, not denominations. Currently one of the big points of tension within the Southern Baptist Convention, the Presbyterian Church (U.S.A.), the Evangelical Lutheran Church in America, The United Methodist Church, the Episcopal Church, and several other American denominations is a product of internal disagreement on whether that denomination should give more weight to legal principles than to shared commitment.

This is NOT a new agenda! The Peace of Augsburg of 1555 and the Treaty of Westphalia of 1648 both attempted to produce a balance between the legal principle and the shared commitment in deciding which would be legitimate Christian bodies in Western Europe. Most, but not all, of the Protestants who emigrated from Europe to America in the seventeenth and eighteenth centuries believed shared commitment should be the central organizing principle in American Christianity.

The highly visible contemporary American example is the contrast between the Roman Catholic Church, which is largely organized around legal principles, and several Baptist traditions, which are organized around shared commitment. Two congregations, one Catholic and one Baptist, each raised $1 million from among the members to construct a new building. Twenty years later both congregations vote to sell their real estate and dissolve. Who receives the money from the sale of that real estate? As a voluntary association that remnant of Baptists who attend the final congregational meeting agree on the next destination of those dollars. The bishop of that Catholic diocese decides how the money received from the sale of that property will be used.

The normal, natural, and predictable trend in American Christianity has been for religious associations initially organized around shared commitment to drift in the direction of placing an increasing reliance on legal principles. The larger the size of the institution, as measured by constituents and/or dollars, the greater the internal institutional pressure to place a heavier emphasis on legal principles. The easy alternative is to shrink in size.

On the surface the paradigm shift recommended in this book appears to be offering congregations a choice between an affinity-based midlevel judicatory and the traditional geographically defined regional judicatory. That is true, but that is only part of the story. The other facet of this recommended paradigm shift calls for minimizing the legal principle and placing a higher value on a voluntary and shared commitment to fulfill the Great Commission.

A review of the history and evolution of political parties, labor unions, and religious systems in America indicates that a focus on shared commitment often results in the creation of a new movement, not a new institution. As long as the central organizing principle continues to be a shared commitment to a specific cause (foreign missions, abolition, prohibition, civil rights), it is relatively easy to attract new adherents. When that movement evolves into a formal organization, the internal pressures inevitably begin to build to rely more and more on legal principles. As legal principles begin to replace that earlier shared commitment as the driving force, a natural, normal, and predictable consequence is more attention is given to identifying the people who should be excluded.

For nearly two thousand years most of the great councils of the Christian church have focused on identifying the people who should be excluded. (See Acts 15:22ff.) That continues as a high priority in American Christianity in the twenty-first century.

Those who are ideologically committed to giving greater weight to the legal principle as the central organizing principle for their denomination can be expected to oppose any changes that will strengthen shared commitment as the central organizing principle. They also will affirm the need to become more exclusionary. In recent years a huge amount of time in American religious organizations has been devoted to identifying the people "we want to exclude." That is a predictable consequence of elevating the influence of legal principles as a central organizing theme. The conflict between those two organizing principles traces back to the Garden of Eden, to the Reformation in Western Europe, and to the affirmation of self-determination as a desirable consequence of affluence. (See chapter 4.)

In summary, if the desired outcome is a denominational system that makes fulfillment of the Great Commission the number-one shared commitment, a probable consequence will be growing pressures from the constituency to minimize the influence of legal principles. The obvious example is instead of telling congregations the name of the midlevel judicatory with which that church will be affiliated, the denomination will ask each congregation to choose that affiliation. Once denominational leaders switch from instructing to asking, it will be difficult to close that door! (For those who are convinced the best alternative is to not open that door, a lot of horses already have left that barn. Instead of sending money to denominational headquarters to support denominationally chosen missionaries sent to other continents, tens of thousands of American Protestant congregations now choose the missionaries they wish to support. Instead of organizing a denominationally designed and related women's organization, thousands of congregations now create their own customized package of ministries with women. Instead of enrolling in a denominationally affiliated theological school, a growing number of candidates for the parish ministry choose a seminary not related to their denomination. Instead of relying on denominational resources for ministries of learning or with youth or in worship, many congregations purchase these services from parachurch organizations.)

Our Way or the Highway?

Four trends in American Protestantism over the past four decades can be cited to summarize this part of the discussion. The first was introduced earlier. The greater the power of legal principles in an organization, the more likely that will be accompanied by decisions to become more exclusionary. The second is the long-term numerical decrease in several denominations in the market share of the American churchgoing population. A third is the natural, normal, and predictable bureaucratic tendency of a declining organization to place greater emphasis on legal principles as the central organizing principle. Given the choice between losing power and losing people, the natural choice is to attempt to retain power. The fourth trend is in that message received by many of the laity, "Our way or the highway." On receipt of that message, a few thousand clergy and millions of laity have already decided to take the highway.

During the nineteenth century the delivery of this ultimatum, "Our way or the highway," led to the creation of several new American Protestant denominations. Will that pattern be repeated in the twenty-first century?

Fuller's Fifth Law

At this point the thirty-year-old reader in excellent health may conclude, "If implementation of the central recommendation in this book depends on my denomination reducing its dependence on legal principles, I've wasted my time! I don't expect to live long enough to see that happen."

That is a realistic observation. The best response can be found in Fuller's Fifth Law on human associations, "As an association moves increasingly toward a situation in which it is dominated by the legal principle, it reaches a stage in which it not only can safely tolerate, but increasingly needs internal groupings that are themselves sustained by the principle of shared commitment."[3] A similar observation about the American scene was made by Alexis de Tocqueville in his book, *Democracy in America* nearly two hundred years ago.

The caucuses, paradenominational agencies, independent ad hoc protest groups, reform movements, and other single-issue organizations that have emerged in several mainline Protestant denominations since 1950 constitute a predictable reaction to the drift toward greater reliance on legal principles. Every denominational merger also is naturally accompanied by an increased reliance on legal principles as a means of overcoming differences in polity and belief systems.

The intuitive response by the leaders in a denominational system increasingly organized around the legal principle will be to oppose any suggestion that calls for the creation of groups organized around a shared commitment. Frequently the sense of an adversarial relationship is increased as the leaders of these new groups identify the denominational policymakers as the enemy. This is a natural human tendency to use that ancient organizing principle to create a closely knit and unified organization out of a group of individuals—identify the enemy and organize against that enemy.[4]

A more productive counterintuitive response to the central recommendation of this book could be, "Fuller's Fifth Law suggests encouraging the creation of affinity judicatories may be necessary for perpetuating the power of our key legal principles."

From Geography to Affinity

A fourth major consequence of adopting and implementing the concept of affinity judicatories requires a different kind of change in one's conceptual framework. Instead of using political subdivisions such as counties and states to define the congregations affiliated with a particular midlevel judicatory, this system replaces geography with affinity. At least a few of these affinity judicatories will include congregations scattered among forty to fifty states. Others will include congregations from several states. Instead of identifying congregations by the location of their meeting place, this system identifies congregations by their distinctive role in ministry.

How much time will be required to persuade people the automobile and low cost air travel have replaced the horse and buggy, the bicycle, and the railroad as the most popular forms of personal transportation in America?

From Top Down to the Grass Roots

For many the most threatening consequence will be the assumption that not only can congregational leaders be trusted, that huge inventory of local leadership also can be a tremendous source of creativity, energy, commitment, time, new ideas, initiative, prayer, innovation, venturesome and future-oriented volunteers, dollars, and professional skills. This has been demonstrated for more than three decades by scores of new nondenominational megachurches.

Challenge the people with the Great Commission and they will respond! Challenge them to help resource someone else's goals, and many will go watch television or surf the Internet. This is an especially common pattern among churchgoers born after 1960. This is only a minor issue with those denominations who have identified people born before 1930 as their primary constituency. Many of the members of those older generations grew up on a culture that taught them to be comfortable with a highly centralized command and control system. Their children and grandchildren, however, were reared in the culture described in chapter 4.

Three Secondary Consequences

In addition to those five institution-threatening changes, three relatively minor consequences merit a word. The most subtle is a change in the source of pain. After a few years a person can adapt to the pain of arthritis in the thumbs. Next comes a sudden toothache. The skill of adapting to one source of pain does not automatically enable a person to be comfortable with a new source of pain. Many denominational leaders have learned how to adapt to the pain created when the annual performance review reports that the proportion of all Christian churchgoers in America worshiping with "our congregations" on the typical weekend is down for the fourteenth or twenty-third consecutive year. The decision to abandon efforts to perpetuate the old in favor of giving birth to the new creates a new source of pain. It is easier to live with the old pain than to adapt to a new pain.

A second consequence will be experienced by those who have enjoyed the intradenominational quarreling that was nurtured by systems that brought together under one geographically defined umbrella people with sharply different values, ideologies, belief systems, dreams, goals, priorities, and definition of what "God is calling our church to be and to be doing." The geographically defined midlevel judicatories provide a fertile environment for intradenominational quarreling. The affinity networks provide a comparatively barren environment for that sport.

It is not irrelevant to note here that one of the motivating forces that led to the organization of the Baptist General Convention of Missouri in mid-2002 was the hope to replace "the strife and conflict of the past" with a focus on fulfilling the Great Commission.[5]

A third, and for some the most frustrating, consequence is the absence of models in American Protestantism that demonstrate how the road to Christian unity overlaps with the road to fulfilling the Great Commission. History suggests those two roads are either at right angles or may even run in opposite directions.

While it may not be openly discussed for several more years, one of the consequences of a change from geographically defined judicatories to affinity judicatories will be the challenge to theological seminaries. Up through the 1940s most American seminaries, both Protestant and Roman Catholic, concentrated on preparing students for either (a) service as parish pastors in that region of the nation in which the seminary was located or (b) service as missionaries on another continent. Most even focused more narrowly on preparing students to serve in one particular religious tradition. The course of study was designed to produce generalists, not specialists.

Today the demand for paid parish staff, both lay and clergy, is for specialists. The creation of affinity judicatories is motivated by the need to affirm and support specialization in response to the demand for higher quality.

One response already in place is for megachurches to enlist future paid staff from among their volunteers in ministry and to provide demanding on-the-job equipping experiences for these new staff members. One part of the explanation is that the key variable in building staff teams is character. The only way we can evaluate a person's character is over a long period of time under varying circumstances. A second reason is "We can teach skills, but more important than skills in seeking new staff, is to choose persons who know, understand, and affirm the distinctive culture of our congregation." A third factor is, "We want team players, not solo performers. The best way to achieve that goal is to choose from among our volunteers those who have been effective and productive in one or more of our ministry teams." Another reason, which some place first, is, "We must have persons on our staff who are deeply devoted followers of Jesus Christ. We do better in achieving that goal by choosing from among our volunteers than we do interviewing seminary graduates."

Another response to that call for specialized staff members, including the clergy, already is in place. While too few in numbers to meet the demand, these are the self-identified teaching churches that "graduate" more equipped specialists than they need for their own ministry. Their "exports" are in great demand by other congregations. The Internet is the new marketplace.

Where and how theological seminaries will respond to this new national, and increasingly interdenominational, market for staff specialists is a story that probably cannot be written before 2015. For several theological schools one alternative is to create an endowment fund of $100 million, more or less, that will free them to create their own future.

While it will affect only several thousand people directly, an inevitable consequence of the paradigm shift recommended in this book is scores of adults will lose their jobs. Many will be able to postpone their departure until the date of retirement (or death) arrives. Others will be eager and able to master new skills. A fair number probably will welcome a return to the parish ministry. A substantial number, however, will find their position is not a part of the new table of organization. That is a common consequence of change. Change produces both winners and losers.

Inventing Tomorrow

Finally, four other probable consequences merit discussion. All four require the gifts, skills, determination, prayers, energy, and creativity of leaders who are comfortable inventing a new tomorrow.

The first of these can be seen more clearly in the secular marketplace. The old American economy was a producer-driven economy. The producers of goods and services decided what they wanted to offer in the marketplace and followed that up by a variety of attempts to persuade consumers to purchase those goods and services. That generalization applied to automobile manufacturers, public high schools, grocery stores, the railroads, hospitals, financial institutions, colleges and universities, five and dime variety stores, park districts, hotels, insurance companies, restaurants, farmers, and churches.

Today the American economy gives far greater weight to the preferences of the customers. One consequence has been the economic failure of millions of enterprises that ignored that change and continued down the producer-driven road. Another is the far greater sensitivity to the expectations, needs, wants, convenience, schedules, and preferences of the customer.

The central recommendation in this book affirms the differences among congregations as well as the differences among people. Several articulate Christian leaders, however, agree that introducing a consumer-driven approach to the organization of denominational systems is ideological heresy and clear proof the devil is alive and at work in this world.

The second of these four has been mentioned earlier. The nineteenth century in the history of American Protestant Christianity was marked by schisms. The twentieth century, especially the post–World War II era, brought a new demand for Christian unity. The last half of the twentieth century also was marked by an unprecedented number of white Protestant American adults gathering weekly for the corporate worship of God.

The historical record, however, is short of examples of denominational systems that chose the road marked, "Christian unity" and also retained their "market share" of Christian churchgoers. The more common pattern was going down the road of Christian unity was accompanied by a net decrease in worship attendance for that denomination.

The current need is for denominational leaders to design and pave a new road that is attractive to two constituencies. One consists of those who place a high value on Christian unity. The second constituency includes those who are convinced every congregation should be organized around the goal of fulfilling the Great Commission and that every facet of their denominational system should be designed to help make that happen. This means that shared commitment to fulfilling the Great Commission must be more influential than legal principles on designing and paving that new road.

The third of these four probable consequences presents another choose-up-sides issue. What is the top priority in the allocation of the discretionary financial resources of a congregation? One response is illustrated by the Seventh-day Adventist Church. Every member is expected to return to the Lord the biblical tithe. That tithe, however, goes to the conference and approximately two-fifths of that tithe is forwarded to a larger regional judicatory and to the national treasury in Maryland. It should be noted that the compensation for pastors as well as for conference staff is paid out of the conference's share of the tithe. The congregations depend on gifts and offerings beyond the tithe to cover their other expenditures.[6]

Several other Protestant denominations ask their congregations to send somewhere between five and forty percent of the congregational receipts to fund the regional and national agencies of that denomination. A couple of denominations define this as the first claim on those discretionary dollars.

A typical pattern in nondenominational congregations is to divide those discretionary dollars among these pots. One pot of money is allocated to efforts to fulfill the Great Commission by other people in other places. The second pot of discretionary dollars is allocated to reinforce and expand the capability of that congregation to fulfill the Great Commission. This may be enlarging the physical facilities or adding new ministries or scheduling and staffing worship and learning ministries at off-campus locations or adopting "wounded birds" (existing congregations that require healing and help to learn to fly by themselves) or sponsoring new missions or other outreach efforts. The third, and largest pot of money is used to fund the annual operating expenses of that congregation.

In several denominational families the current system forces people to choose up sides. On one side are those who believe that one of the top reasons for the existence of congregations is to collect and send money to denominational headquarters. On the other side are those who are convinced that in the new American economy denominational agencies can and should depend on a variety of income streams to pay their bills. These streams include (a) fees for services, (b) bequests, (c) gifts from individuals, (d) gifts from family foundations, (e) investment income, (f) responses through designated second-mile financial contributions to precisely defined mission ventures such as new church development, and (g) the sale of resources.[7]

Finally, the most critical variable in designing a renewal strategy for any aging institution is in the criteria used to choose the people who will design the strategy and those who will implement that strategy. Which forces will drive the deliberations of that leadership group? Will the desire to fulfill the Great Commission be the number-one variable in selecting the people who will participate in those deliberations? Or will the focus be on choosing members who are deeply committed to perpetuating denominational traditions? Or policymakers who believe the call to Christian unity should drive that planning process? Or those who believe the crucial need is to strengthen the legal principles that shape the culture of that religious body? Or those who believe the top priority is to improve the survival possibilities for small membership congregations? Or will the formula for selection require one from that caucus, one from that special interest group, two from that category, one from that lobby, one from that board in order to represent the demographic diversity, the regional differences, and the ideological pluralism of the denomination?

In summary, is the alternative of encouraging congregations to create new affinity judicatories to supplement or replace the traditional geographically defined midlevel judicatories a fantasy or a real possibility?

The answer to that question probably will be determined by three variables. First is the capability for meaningful internal self-criticism. Second is the degree of openness to change. Third will be the criteria used to select the members of that ad hoc task force charged with designing a strategy for the renewal of that denomination.

APPENDIX A

HOW MANY ARE COMPETITIVE?

I f we agree that an American Protestant congregation (a) requires a full-time and fully credentialed resident pastor to be able to compete effectively with other churches in its efforts to reach, attract, serve, and assimilate new generations of churchgoers and (b) requires the capability to attract, challenge, retain, and financially afford a full-time and fully credentialed and resident pastor requires an average weekend worship attendance of more than 125, what proportion of the congregations in any one denomination meet that standard?

In many urban and suburban communities pastors contend an average worship attendance of more than 350 is required for a Protestant congregation to be able to compete in efforts to reach the generations of churchgoers born after 1950.

WHO IS COMPETITIVE?

Proportion of Congregations Reporting Average Worship Attendance Exceeds

Denomination	126+ Average Attendance	351+ Average Attendance
Evangelical Free Church in America	51%	16%
Evangelical Lutheran Church in America	44%	8%
Baptist General Conference	41%	12%
Presbyterian Church in America	37%`	9%
Episcopal Church	31%	5%
Assemblies of God	29%	7%
Southern Baptist Convention	28%	7%
Presbyterian Church (USA)	26%	5%
United Church of Christ	24%	2%
Disciples of Christ	23%	*
United Methodist	22%	3%
American Baptist Churches	21%	*

* = Less than 2 percent

In designing the organizational system for your denomination for the twenty-first century, what is one of the desired outcomes? That more than one-half of all congregations will average more than 125 at worship? If only one-fourth reach that standard, is that an acceptable outcome?

Or do you believe a reasonable outcome is that at least 10 percent of all congregations will average more than 350 at worship? What do you believe is the minimum size to be competitive in this increasingly competitive ecclesiastical environment?

WHAT IS THE MEDIAN?

The median is the number that separates the larger half from the smaller half in an array of numbers. For example, the median age of the American population in April 2000 was 36.5 years, up from a median age of 32.8 years in 1990 and 30.0 years in 1980.

In recent years a variety of surveys of American Protestant congregations have suggested that median number for average worship attendance is somewhere between ninety and one hundred.

A different methodology relies on the reports by congregations to their denominational headquarters. In recent years an increasing number of denominations have been asking for the average worship attendance in congregational reports. The proportion of congregations including that number in their annual reports usually ranges between 85 percent and 97 percent. When the numbers from the "no report" churches are examined, the reported membership figures reveal that most of the congregations not reporting their average worship attendance report fewer than fifty members. That suggests significant under-reporting in the proportions of small congregations.

We also lack adequate data on worship attendance in that growing number of nondenominational house churches, or that huge variety of independent churches ranging in size from small storefront congregations with fewer than a dozen worshipers to nondenominational megachurches averaging more than five thousand in weekend attendance.

What do we have? We do have reasonably reliable data from several denominations that together include approximately 145,000 congregations. This database includes the average weekly worship attendance. These averages suggest the median average worship attendance of all American Protestant congregations is close to seventy since the largest denominations are clustered near or below seventy.

Denomination	Average Attendance	Denomination	Average Attendance
Lutheran Church-Missour Synod	125	United Church Christ	82*
Evangelical Free Church	115	Episcopal Church	78
Baptist General Conference	110	Southern Baptist Convention	76
Evangelical Lutheran Church in America	100	Assemblies of God	70
Presyterian Chuch in America	98	Presbyterian Church (U.S.A.)	68
Evengelical Covenant Church	96	The United Methodist Church	55
Wisconsin Evangelical Lutheran Synod	95		

*A large proportion of small membership UCC congregations did not report their average worship attendance.

WHAT IS THE MODE?

In statistical terms the word "average" has three definitions. Frequently the most useful is the median—one-half of all items in that statistical array fall above the median and one-half fall below the median. A second is the means. See appendix B. All of the numbers in that statistical array are added together, and the sum is divided by the total number of items in that array. That can have misleading conclusions. For example, if there are eleven congregations affiliated with your denomination, what is their average size? Last week one reported an average attendance of one hundred, two reported an average of 150, two reported an average of two hundred, one reported an average of three hundred, four reported an average of 325, and one reported an average worship attendance of two thousand.

The median average worship attendance was three hundred. Five averaged fewer than three hundred at worship, and five averaged more than three hundred at worship. The mean average was (4,400 divided by eleven) four hundred, but only one of the eleven reached that average.

That introduces the third definition. That is the mode, the number that occurs most frequently in an array of numbers. In this example, the mode is an average worship attendance of 325. In September in that elementary school classroom filled with two dozen first graders plus one fifty-six-year-old teacher, the median age is six years, the mode also is six, but the mean is nearly thirty-four—and no one in the room is even close to that "average" age!

What are the most frequently reported numbers when congregations report their worship attendance?

The Southern Baptist Convention represents the typical distribution. A total of 1004 Southern Baptist congregations reported worship attendance of 40 on the last Sunday in September 1999. (That represents the SBC reporting system.) Another 851 reported 30, 791 reported 350, and 680 reported 25.

The mode for the Presbyterian Church (U.S.A.) in 2001 was 269 congregations reporting an average worship attendance of 40 followed by 237 congregations reporting 30, 233 reporting 35, and 205 reporting 20.

The mode for the Assemblies of God, which has more of a large church orientation, was 40 reported by 380 congregations. Another 365 reported an average worship attendance of 50, 353 reported 75, 346 reported 60, and 333 reported 30.

In 1999, 846 United Methodist congregations reported an average worship attendance of 30, 842 reported 35, 837 reported 25, 802 reported 20, while 782 reported 60, and 644 reported 15. In the Episcopal Church USA 74 parishes reported an average worship attendance of 30 for 2000 while 72 reported 72, 66 reported 22, 65 reported 35, another 65 reported 40, and another 65 reported 20.

The five most frequently reported numbers in the Presbyterian Church in America were an average worship attendance of 50 by 38 congregations, 75 by 36, 60 by another 36, 80 by 34, and 100 by 31 churches.

APPENDIX D

WHAT PROPORTION ARE SMALL CONGREGATIONS?

When American Protestant congregations are asked to report their average worship attendance, the most frequently reported numbers usually are 20, 25, 30, 35, and 40, although not necessarily in that order of frequency. For United Methodists, for example, the most frequently reported number is 35 while for the Baptist General Conference it is 25 and 40 for the Presbyterian Church (U.S.A.).

Why so small? The core of the explanation is if one places a high value on the importance of interpersonal relationships among the members of that group, the *maximum* number of participants is between twenty and forty. That point is illustrated by the number of students in an elementary school classroom, by the number of players on the active roster on a professional baseball team, by three thousand years of military formations, by adult Sunday school classes, by most church choirs, and by family reunions. The big exceptions are those groups in which the members are expected to make personal sacrifices to advance the best interests of that group. The ideal size for these groups varies from five to twelve, but usually it is a single digit number in the three-to-seven range.

What proportion of the congregations in your denomination report an average worship attendance of fewer than twenty-five? The larger that percentage, the more likely your denomination has been experiencing an aging and numerical decrease among the constituents. Why? Because American Protestant churchgoers born after 1960 can be found in disproportionately large numbers in congregations averaging more than five hundred at worship.

What proportion of congregations report an average worship attendance fewer than twenty-five? The range is huge!

Denomination	Percentage Reporting Average Worship Attendance of Less than 25
The United Methodist Church	19%
Episcopal Church	15%
Disciples of Christ	11%
Presbyterian Church (U.S.A.)	11%
Assemblies of God	11%
Southern Baptist Convention	9%
United Church of Christ	7%
American Baptist Churches	7%
Presbyterian Church in Am.	6%
Wisconsin Evangelical Lutheran Synod	6%
Evangelical Lutheran Church in Am.	6%
Lutheran Church-Missouri Synod	4%
Baptist General Conference	3%
Evangelical Covenant Church	3%
Evangelical Free Church of America	1%

WHAT PROPORTION ARE LARGE CONGREGATIONS?

I n those denominational families that have been asking congregations to report their average attendance at weekend worship, two trends repeatedly appear. One is during the 1990s the majority of congregations reporting an average attendance less than one hundred (or sometimes under 150) in 1990 experienced a decrease in attendance during the 1990s. A second common trend is a majority, and usually a substantial majority, of those congregations reporting an average worship attendance of more than five hundred in 1990 reported an increase during the 1990s.

This suggests that the large churches are more likely to be able to attract new constituents than are the small congregations in what has become a highly competitive ecclesiastical marketplace. A related trend is those denominations with a relatively small proportion of large congregations are most likely to report a shrinking constituency. What is the range? These figures represent the proportion of congregations in that denomination that reported an average worship attendance of more than five hundred in 2000.

Denomination	Percentage Reporting Average Worship Attendance of More than 500
Evangelical Presbyterian Church	10%
Evangelical Free Church in America	8%
Baptist General Conference	7%
Presbyterian Church in America	6%
Lutheran Church-Missouri Synod	5%
Wisconsin Evangelical Lutheran Synod	5%
Assemblies of God	4%
Southern Baptist Convention	4%
Evangelical Covenant Church	3%
Evangelical Lutheran Church in America	3%
Presbyterian Church (U.S.A.)	2.3%
The United Methodist Church	2.1%
Episcopal Church	2%
American Baptist Churches	1.3%
United Church of Christ	0.7%
Disciples of Christ	0.5%

APPENDIX F

THAT BIG CHURCH PLANTING BOOM

The most comprehensive census of religious congregations ever completed in the United States was conducted by the United States Bureau of the Census for 1906 and published in 1910. Among the many questions asked was the date of organization for each congregation. Approximately 85 percent of all churches provided that date, so the data below do not represent a complete count. A reasonable guess, however, is most of those not reporting that date were organized before 1850. In addition these statistics do not include those congregations organized in the latter decades of the nineteenth century that had disappeared from the scene before 1906. These numbers include only those congregations that were in existence when that census of 1906 was conducted.

What did that census of churches reveal? Among the many conclusions is the 1870–1906 era was the greatest period of church planting in American history! During the 1880s, for example, on the average day nine new Protestant congregations were organized. In a typical year during the 1880s one new Protestant church was organized for every sixteen thousand residents of this nation. To achieve that goal today would require planting at least seventeen thousand new churches annually. (The actual total in 2002 was closer to four thousand.)

For that longer period of 1870 through 1906 inclusive, a total of 124,000 religious congregations were organized. Together they accounted for 58 percent of all congregations counted by that census. That means in 1906 one-half of all religious congregations in America had been organized during the previous thirty-five years!

Five Christian traditions accounted for seven out of ten of all the congregations founded during those thirty-seven years. Sixteen different Baptist denominations organized a combined total of 35,570 new congregations. The fifteen different Methodist denominations accounted for a combined total of 33,133, the twenty-four Lutheran bodies started a combined total of 8,946, the twelve Presbyterian denominations organized a combined total of 8,154, and the Roman Catholic Church in America launched 7,540 new parishes.

In several cases denominational mergers make it impossible to translate those numbers into contemporary denominational systems. The Evangelical Lutheran Synodical Conference of America, for example, reported in 1906 that 2,460 of its 3,301 congregations had been organized during those thirty-seven years, an average of 66.5 per year. Second in size and activity among those two dozen Lutheran bodies was the General Council of the Evangelical Lutheran Church in North America that reported that 1,445 of its 2,148 congregations in 1906 had been organized during that same period.

The Presbyterian Church in the United States of America reported in 1906 that of its 7,935 congregations a total of 4,287 had been organized in that 1870–1906 era while the Presbyterian Church in the United States reported 1,524 of its 3,104 congregations were founded during those thirty-seven years, and the Cumberland Presbyterians organized another 1,439 new churches.

Perhaps the best way to provide comparisons among the predecessor of today's mainline Protestant denominations is to convert those totals for that thirty-seven year period into annual averages.

Average Number of Congregations Organized Annually 1870–1906

Denomination	Number	Denomination	Number
The United Methodist Church*	714	African Methodist Episcopal Church	43
National Baptist Convention	416	Seventh-day Adventist	42
Southern Baptist Convention	350	Independent Churches	24
24 Lutheran Bodies	242	Society of Friends	20
Presbyterian Church (U.S.A.)**	208	Salvation Army	19
Roman Catholic Church	204	Unitarian-Universalist	12
United Church of Christ***	128	Advent Christian Church	10

Denomination	Number	Denomination	Number
African Methodist Episcopal Church	126	Reformed Church in America	7
Disciples of Christ	120	Evangelical Covenant Church	7
American Baptist Churches	111	Christian Reformed Church	4
Episcopal Church	101	Evangelical Free Church	3
Christian Methodist Episcopal Church	51	Mennonite Church	2

*Six predecessor denominations
**Four predecessor denominations
***Four predecessor denominations

APPENDIX G

WHERE DO PROTESTANTS GO TO CHURCH?

Nearly nine decades ago an Italian economist and sociologist, Vilfredo Pareto, concluded that a natural distribution pattern in society followed an 80-20 ratio. Contemporary examples include 80 percent of a bank's deposits are made by 20 percent of the customers, 20 percent of prescription drugs account for 80 percent of all prescriptions written by physicians, and 80 percent of a newspaper's revenues from advertising come from 20 percent of the advertisers. While that 80-20 rule does not always reflect contemporary reality, it is a widely quoted guideline.

One exception is contemporary American Protestantism where the 70-30 rule is more common. Give or take a percentage point or two on either side of the equation, large American Protestant congregations report that 70 percent of their financial contributions from living donors come from 30 percent of their current households. Approximately 30 percent of all Americans, age eighteen and over, worship with a religious congregation on the typical weekend. Slightly more than 30 percent of all adult American Christians have switched their denominational affiliation at least once. Slightly more than 30 percent of all adult Americans, according to the Gallup Organization, identify themselves as Baptists.

In those American Protestant denominations that ask congregations to report their worship attendance, give or take one or two percentage points, the smallest 70 percent of the reporting congregations account for 30 percent of the worshipers on the typical weekend while the largest 30 percent account for the other 70 percent. (In the Assemblies of God, for example, the smallest 71 percent of congregations account for 27 percent of the worshipers. In the Southern Baptist Convention, the smallest 70 percent account for 30 percent of the worshipers on that reporting date in September. In The United Methodist Church 70 percent of the reporting congregations report an average worship attendance of fewer than 97, and they account for 33 percent of the total weekend worship attendance in that denomination. In the Episcopal Church USA 29 percent of the congregations report an average worship attendance of 125 or more and accounted for 68 percent of the worshipers.)

A second common pattern is the largest 1 percent of American Protestant congregations account for 9 to 12 percent of the worshipers in churches affiliated with that denomination on the typical weekend. In a few exceptions, such as the Evangelical Covenant Church, the Presbyterian Church in America, the Evangelical Presbyterian Church, and the Assemblies of God, the largest 1 percent account for 12 to 15 percent of worshipers while in a few "small church" and "midsized" church traditions that include relatively few very large congregations, the largest 1 percent account for only 7 to 9 percent of the worshipers.

NOTES

Introduction

1. For an earlier optimistic view of Christianity in America, see the special issue of *Life*, December 26, 1955, especially pages 46-57. For a brief but thoughtful analysis by a contemporary scholar, see Corwin Smidt, "The Future of Denominations," *The Banner*, April 23, 2001, 20-21.

2. Among the scores of excellent books that describe how the Protestant church of the future is being invented in America, five stand out as especially valuable: Donald E. Miller, *Reinventing American Protestantism* (Berkeley: University of California Press, 1997); Adam Hamilton, *Leading Beyond the Walls* (Nashville: Abingdon Press, 2002); B. Carlisle Driggers, *A Journey of Faith and Hope* (Columbia, S.C.: The R. L. Bryan Company, 2000); Michael Slaughter, *Spiritual Entrepreneurs* (Nashville: Abingdon Press, 1995); Claude E. Payne and Hamilton Beazley, *Reclaiming the Great Commission* (San Francisco: Jossey-Bass, 2000).

3. The practice of medicine, like the practice of ministry, is based on hope. The hopeless will not make the best recruits in a crusade to reform any institution from within. The hopeless are more likely to be attracted to revolution than to reform. The recommendations in this book are based on hope. Hope is NOT a synonym for optimism! Kathleen Foley's simple definiton of hope ". . . the certainty that something makes sense," also describes this observer's worldview. That quotation from Vaclav Havel comes from a superb essay by Sherwin B. Nuland, "The Principle of Hope,"

The New Republic, May 27, 2002, 25-30. The first six columns of this essay should be required reading for anyone hoping to help reform any institution from within. A fascinating thesis by an anthropologist that declares optimism is a natural human characteristic is Lionel Tiger, *Optimism: The Biology of Hope* (New York: Simon & Schuster, 1979).

Chapter One: Should You Read This Book?

1. For a provocative discussion of the state of freedom in contemporary America, see the presidential address to the American Historical Association by Eric Foner, "American Freedom in a Global Age," *American Historical Review*, vol. 106, no. 4, Feb. 2001, 1-16.

2. For an introduction to Deming's work see Mary Walton, *The Deming Management Method* (New York: The Putnam Publishing Group, 1986).

3. Lyle E. Schaller, *The Very Large Church* (Nashville: Abingdon Press, 2000).

Chapter Two: Why Talk About It?

1. Milton J. Coalter, John M. Mulder, and Louis B. Weeks, *Vital Signs: The Promise of Mainstream Protestantism* (Grand Rapids, Mich.: William B. Eerdmans Publishing Co., 1996), 99.

2. Ibid., 107.

3. Ibid., 124.

4. Lyle E. Schaller, *What Have We Learned?* (Nashville: Abingdon Press, 2001), 119-123.

5. John A. Byrne, "How to Fix Corporate Governance," *Business Week*, May 6, 2002, 69-71.

6. This trend by the mainline Protestant denominations in America to cut back in planting new missions was described by Lyle E. Schaller, *The Coming Crisis in New Church Development* (Cleveland: Regional Church Planning Office, 1967). This was one of six reports published in the late 1960s to encourage church planting. Between 1970–74, for example, the recently created United Methodist Church averaged only twenty new churches a year compared to an annual average of 175 between 1961–63, and that yearly average of 735 for the six predecessor denominations in the 1880s.

Chapter Three: What Do You Believe?

1. Roger Finke and Rodney Stark, "How the Upstart Sects Won America: 1776–1850," *Journal for the Scientific Study of Religion*, vol. 28, no. 1, 1989, 27-44.

2. Roger Finke and Rodney Stark, *The Churching of America 1776–1990* (New Brunswick, N.J.: Rutgers University Press, 1992), 237-75.

3. Ibid., 248.

4. Alan Wolfe, *One Nation, After All* (New York: Penguin Group, 1986).

Chapter Four: What Are the Consequences of Affluence?

1. The impact on ecclesiastical systems of the increased competition for the charitable dollar is the central theme of Lyle E. Schaller, *The New Context for Ministry* (Nashville: Abingdon Press, 2002), 105-320.

2. Pam Belluck, "Maine Parish Agonizes over a Priest's Confession," *New York Times*, March 5, 2002, 1.

3. What to do with fourteen-year-olds is a major theme of Lyle E. Schaller, *The Evolution of the American Public High School* (Nashville: Abingdon Press, 2002) and David Nasaw, *Schooled to Order* (New York: Oxford University Press, 1979).

4. One perspective on this issue is offered by a trustee of a state university. See Candace de Russy, "Rule By Those of Little Faith," *The Chronicle of Higher Education*, February 22, 2002, B11-13. Another is Alan Wolfe, "Faith and Diversity in American Religion," *The Chronicle of Higher Education*, February 8, 2002, B7-10.

5. Robert L. Randall, *What People Expect from Church* (Nashville: Abingdon Press, 1992).

6. For many years The New York Times Company Foundation has sought contributions for its "Neediest Cases Fund," an antipoverty cause. That foundation knows how to raise money to help those in need. On September 12, 2001, it launched an appeal to help the victims of the previous day's disaster. On the basis of past experience it was expected readers would contribute between $4 million and $5 million. Six months later receipts totaled nearly $60 million despite the competition from more than 190 other funds raising money for the same cause.

7. Nathan Glazer and Daniel Patrick Moynihan, *Beyond the Melting Pot* (Cambridge, Mass.: The M.I.T. Press and Harvard University Press, 1963).

8. Alvin Toffler, *Future Shock* (New York: Random House, 1970), 325-28.

9. For alternative strategies to create a multicultural denomination, see Lyle E. Schaller, *What Have We Learned?* (Nashville: Abingdon Press, 2001), 197-213.

10. If the pastor decides to force the congregation to choose between supporting "our minister" and alienating a key family in that small congregation,

most members will prefer to ignore that demand. If forced to make a choice, the easier alternative is to bid the pastor farewell.

11. An interesting study book that summarized this plea was published in the middle of the twentieth century, Robert S. Bilheimer, et al. *The Quest for Christian Unity* (New York: Association Press, 1952).

12. This battle between customization and expertise is described in Jan Parker, "Fast Food," *The New Yorker*, May 27, 2002, 70-75.

13. In 1955 there were at least forty-five million Americans, age fourteen and over, who attended a Christian worship service on at least twenty-six weekends in that year. The most significant factor behind the changes in church attendance patterns since 1955 has been death. Most of those regular churchgoers of 1955 are dead. Two revealing research reports that explain why their children did not replace them in church are Dean R. Hoge, Benton Johnson, and Donald A. Luidens, *Vanishing Boundaries* (Louisville: Westminster/John Knox Press, 1994); and Dean R. Hoge et al., *Young Adult Catholics* (South Bend: University of Notre Dame Press, 2001).

14. John Kenneth Galbraith, *The Affluent Society* (Boston: Houghton Mifflin, 1958), 40-43, 61-63, 100-6, 216-19.

Chapter Six: What Are the Desired Outcomes?

1. A superb case study of the value of research in producing happy customers is the evolution of the disposable diaper. See Malcolm Gladwell, "Smaller," *The New Yorker*, Nov. 26, 2001, 74-79.

2. The future of traditional denominational systems in American Protestantism has been the subject of many books with more to come. Among the most useful were: George Marsden, *Fundamentalism and American Culture* (New York: Oxford University Press, 1980); Robert William Fogel, *The Fourth Great Awakening* (Chicago: University of Chicago Press, 2000); Wade Clark Roof and William McKinley, *American Mainline Religion* (New Brunswick, N.J.: Rutgers University Press, 1987); Donald E. Miller, *Reinventing American Protestantism* (Los Angeles: University of California Press, 1997); Robert Bruce Mullin and Russell E. Richey, eds., *Reimagining Denominationalism* (New York: Oxford University Press, 1994); William R. Hutchison, editor, *Between the Times* (New York: Cambridge University Press, 1989); David A. Roozen and C. Kirk Hadaway, eds., *Church and Denominational Growth* (Nashville: Abingdon Press, 1993); Christian Smith, *American Evangelicalism* (Chicago: University of Chicago Press, 1998); Jackson Carroll and Wade Clark Roof, eds., *Beyond Establishment* (Louisville: Westminister/John Knox Press, 1993); James Davison Hunter, *Culture Wars* (New York: Basic Books, 1991); Joel A. Carpenter, *Revive Us*

Again (New York: Oxford University Press, 1997); C. Eric Lincoln and Lawrence H. Mameya, *The Black Church in the African American Experience* (Durham, N.C.: Duke University Press, 1991); Paul K. Conklin, *American Originals* (Chapel Hill, N.C.: University of North Carolina Press, 1997); Ellen M. Roseberg, *The Southern Baptists: A Subculture in Transition* (Knoxville, Tenn: University of Tennessee Press, 1989); Nathan O. Hatch, *The Democratization of American Christianity* (New Haven: Yale University Press, 1989); and R. Stephen Warner, *New Wine in Old Wineskins* (Los Angeles: University of California Press, 1988). It is interesting to note that ten of these fourteen books were published by university presses.

From this pilgrim's perspective the most provocative is Roger Finke and Rodney Stark, *The Churching of America* (New Brunswick, N.J.: Rutgers University Press, 1992). United Methodists may want to read A. Gregory Schneider, *The Way of the Cross Leads Home* (Bloomington: Indiana University Press, 1993); Russell E. Richey, *The Methodist Conference in America* (Nashville: Kingswood Books, 1996); Russell E. Richey et al., eds., *Questions for the Twenty-First Century Church* (Nashville: Abingdon Press, 1999); Douglas W. Johnson and Alan K. Waltz, *Facts and Possibilities* (Nashville: Abingdon Press, 1987); Lyle E. Schaller, *Tattered Trust* (Nashville: Abingdon Press, 1996); and the seventeen-volume series, *Into Our Third Century*, edited by Alan K. Waltz and Ezra Earl Jones and published by Abingdon Press, 1980–83.

As usual the Presbyterians were ahead of everyone else in anticipating the future. The multivolume series, *The Presbyterian Presence: The Twentieth Century Experience*, eds. Milton J. Coalter, John M. Mulder, and Louis B. Weeks (Louisville: Westminster/John Knox Press, 1990–92) continues to be a gold mine of relevant research and insights. Concurrently the relatively new Presbyterian Church in America has adopted new church development as its central organizing principle while the even newer Evangelical Presbyterian Church has become the most compatible Protestant denominational environment for very large congregations.

Chapter Seven: What About the Polity?

1. Robert William Fogel, *The Fourth Great Awakening and the Future of Egalitarianism* (Chicago: University of Chicago Press, 2000).

2. Nathan O. Hatch, *The Democratization of American Christianity* (New Haven: Yale University Press, 1989). Another fascinating story is Frederick V. Mills, Sr., *Bishops by Ballot* (New York: Oxford University Press, 1978).

3. For a brief reflection on this trend, see Martin E. Marty, "Bishoping," *The Christian Century*, February 13-20, 2002, 79.

4. This role is described in operational terms in Lyle E. Schaller, *The New Context for Ministry* (Nashville: Abingdon Press, 2002), 273-312.

5. For an informative and provocative discussion of the regulatory role, see Craig Dykstra and James Hudnut-Beumler, "The National Organizational Structure of Protestant Denominations: An Invitation to a Conversation" in *The Organizational Revolution*, edited by Milton J. Coalter et al. (Louisville: Westminster/John Knox Press, 1992), 307-31. An excellent explanation of the power of tradition and polity that also describes the tensions created by combining a made-in-America religious body with a Western European religious heritage is W. Widick Schroeder, "The United Church of Christ: The Quest for Denominational Identity and the Limits of Pluralism" in Dorothy C. Bass and Kenneth B. Smith, eds., *The United Church of Christ: Studies in Identity and Polity* (Chicago: Exploration Press, 1987), 15-33.

6. A superb resource on this subject is *Voluntary Associations* eds. J. Roland Pennock and John W. Chapman (New York: Atherton Press, 1969). See chapter 8 for a longer discussion of this topic.

Chapter Eight: What Is Your Frame of Reference?

1. Rosabeth Moss Kanter, "Strategy as Improvisational Theater," *MIT Sloan Management Review*, Winter 2002, 76-81.

Chapter Ten: Twelve Alternative Scenarios

1. B. Carlyle Driggers, *A Journey of Faith and Hope* (Columbia, S.C.: The R. L. Bryan Company, 2000).

2. Claude E. Payne and Hamilton Beazley, *Reclaiming the Great Commission* (San Francisco: Jossey-Bass, 2000).

3. Keith B. Brown, *On the Road Again* (New York: Church Publishing, 2001), 116.

Chapter Eleven: A Third Paradigm Shift

1. Matthew Boyle, "The Right Stuff," *Fortune*, March 4, 2000, 85-87.

Chapter Twelve: Trade-offs and Consequences

1. An exceptionally valuable essay on this distinction between the voluntary association organized around a shared commitment of the members and the one organized around the legal principle is, "Two Principles of

Human Association" in *Voluntary Associations*, eds. J. Roland Pennock and John W. Chapman (New York: Atherton Press, 1969), 3-23.

2. Ibid., 12.

3. Ibid., 13.

4. This ancient organizing principle is described in Lyle E. Schaller, *Community Organization: Conflict and Reconciliation* (Nashville: Abingdon Press, 1965), 49-114.

5. Bob Allen, "New Missouri convention vows to shun Baptist politics," *Baptist Standard*, April 29, 2002, 3.

6. Decades of experience suggest this system of paying parish pastors out of a central treasury is most compatible with a denominational system with an institutional value system that (a) affirms short pastorates of two-to-five years, (b) prefers small and midsized congregations rather than large churches, (c) places a high value on perpetuating the old rather than on creating the new, (d) displays a high level of trust in denominational officials and a lower level of trust in congregational leaders, (e) uses a reward system that places denominational loyalty above creativity and entrepreneurial gifts, (f) is more comfortable with a socialist economy than with a capitalist economy, (g) gives greater weight to legal principles than to a shared commitment as the central organizing principle, and (h) places a low value on continuity being in the leadership and a high value on continuity being in the institution.

7. For a more extensive discussion of how to fund denominational systems in the twenty-first century see Lyle E. Schaller, *The New Context for Ministry* (Nashville: Abingdon Press, 2002), 273-312.